WORTH DYING FOR

SACRIFICE, SUCCESS, AND SUBMITTING TO LIFE'S GREATEST TRUTH

L. TODD KELLY

ADVANCE PRAISES

AS A PASTOR, I am well acquainted with the concept of redemption. In fact, I often have a front row seat to see how immeasurable grace can completely transform a person. That couldn't be truer of L. Todd Kelly. His story is truly a redemption story. Whether on the battlefield of life or in the battlefield of the courtroom, Todd has always given his all, but this book shows how our all is often not enough. And it's in those places where we can come face to face with our humanity, and face to face with our Redeemer. I pray that this book challenges you and I pray it's a blessing to you, just as Todd has been in my life.

~ Joe Champion,
Senior Pastor of Celebration Church in Austin, TX
Author of Confronting Compromise

TODD HAS EXPOSED a truth in our culture about the demons that can control us if we let them His revelation about the impact that those demons had on his law practice, his marriage, and his family are too often hidden and allowed to grow, unchecked, in society, and especially in the world of the trial lawyer As a fellow trial lawyer, I have seen first-hand the destructive powers that Todd faced, and watched too many succumb to them This book is a must-read for trial lawyers, new and old, but is also an in-depth exploration for so many others to enjoy I commend this book to your collection with enthusiasm.

~ Mikal C. Watts, Esq., Trial Lawyer

L. TODD KELLY'S Book is a must read! It is amazingly raw, authentic and Todd is extremely transparent throughout this book I could not put the book down once I started it If you have ever felt pain, then this book is for you. Thirty years ago, I was feeling so much pain that I tried to end my own life after working undercover for the FBI for three long years, wearing a wire every day. This book will show you that most of us have some dark periods in our life, but that there is HOPE at the end of the journey. I wish that I had this book available thirty years ago. It would have made a significant difference. I highly recommend L. Todd Kelly's book!

~ Mark Whitacre, PhD.
Subject of the movie, ***The Informant****,*
(Matt Damon played Mark Whitacre)
Executive Director, t-factor, at Coca-Cola Consolidated, Inc.

L. TODD KELLY IS a gifted trial lawyer, a former Marine officer, a loving father and husband and a dedicated follower of Christ. Todd's life demonstrates learning from your mistakes at a level I have never witnessed; he is now sharing his life story to impact and save the lives of others. Todd is living proof that the power of God can transform any situation and I salute him for having the courage to write this book. Suicide has reached epidemic levels in our country. His powerful book is timely, needed and can change your life! I consider it a must read for anyone.

~Ken Schiller, Entrepreneur
Malcom Baldrige Recipient & Malcom Baldrige Judge
Suicide Crisis Hotline Volunteer

As someone who has walked a mile in Todd Kelly's shoes, I can say with absolute conviction that his memoir, "Worth Dying For," is a must-read for anyone who has ever faced their own demons and struggled to find the light. Todd's journey from the depths of despair, contemplating ending it all, to finding renewed strength and purpose through his faith in Jesus Christ, is a testament to the resilience of the human spirit and the transformative power of God's love.

When I wrote my song "God or the Gun," I poured my own pain and struggles into those lyrics, just as Todd has poured his heart and soul onto these pages. The parallels between our stories are striking - the feelings of worthlessness, the sense that we had failed those we loved most, the desperation that drives a person to the brink of suicide. But what resonated with me most was Todd's ultimate realization that his life had value, that he was precious in the eyes of God.

There's a line in "Worth Dying For" that struck me like a lightning bolt: "I NOW UNDERSTAND THAT TO JESUS, I, LIKE YOU, WAS WORTH DYING FOR." Those words encapsulate the very core of the Christian message - that no matter how far we may stray, no matter how lost we may feel, we are never beyond the reach of God's grace and redemption. Todd's story is a powerful reminder of that truth.

Through his raw honesty and unflinching self-reflection, Todd invites us to confront our own struggles and doubts, and to find strength in the knowledge that we are not alone. His journey from the courtroom to the depths of his own soul and back again is both gripping and inspiring. You'll find yourself cheering for him as he takes on corporate giants and fights for justice, and weeping with him as he hits rock bottom and wonders if he has the strength to carry on.

But carry on he does, "Worth Dying For" is more than just a memoir - it's a roadmap for the soul, a beacon of light for anyone who has ever felt lost or broken.

~ Ty Herndon, American Country Music Singer and Songwriter

Heroes, everyone needs one, but no one knows the price you pay to be one until the bill comes due. L. Todd Kelly's book "Worth Dying For" outlines the high price paid by those who choose to stand in the gap.

As the mother of a first responder and someone who runs a ministry for at-risk youth, I felt the pain emanating off the page and know the high price that is exacted physically and mentally for those who choose to champion the causes of others.

This book also highlights the cost demanded from the ones who love these heroes the most, the forgotten support behind the cape. It pays honor to those who hold up the arms, keep meals warm and create a soft place for heroes to land.

What a beautiful story of redemption through surrender. We find that it is in turning over everything to the One who is able to sustain the hero and carry the weight that they can be free to do what they were created to do.

~ Lorie Goggin
Executive Director of Reset Mentoring

WORTH DYING FOR

SACRIFICE, SUCCESS, AND SUBMITTING TO LIFE'S GREATEST TRUTH

L. TODD KELLY

Worth Dying For: Sacrifice, Success, and Submitting to Life's Greatest Truth
Copyright © 2023 -2024 L. Todd Kelly.

The conversations in the book all come from the author's recollections, though they are not written to represent word-for-word transcripts. Rather, the author has retold them in a way that evokes the feeling and meaning of what was said, and, in all instances, the essence of dialogue is accurate.

This is a work of creative nonfiction. The events are portrayed to the best of L. Todd Kelly's memory. While all the stories in this book are true, some names and identifying details may have been changed to protect the privacy of the people involved.

All rights reserved. No part of this publication may be reproduced, distributed, or transmitted in any form or by any means, including photocopying, recording, or other electronic or mechanical methods, without the prior written permission of the publisher, except in the case of brief quotations embodied in critical reviews and certain other noncommercial uses permitted by copyright law.

For permission requests, write to the publisher, addressed "Attention: Permissions Coordinator," at the address below.

ISBN: 979-8-9899782-0-5 (Paperback)
ISBN: 979-8-9899782-1-2 (Hardcover)
ISBN: 979-8-9899782-2-9 (Digital/Kindle)
ISBN: 979-8-9899782-3-6 (Audio)
ISBN: 979-8-9899782-4-3 (Hardback/Barnes & Noble)

Front cover image by Nick Austin
Book design by Ali Craig
Printed in the United States of America.

Victor + Valor
4500 Williams Dr Ste212-421
Georgetown. TX 78633
https://www.victorvalor.org/

First Printing: 2024
10 9 8 7 6 5 4 3 2 1

THIS BOOK IS for anyone who has ever experienced pain on someone else's behalf—especially trial lawyers (who do it daily).

I dedicate this book to my Lord, the God of the Universe, who has saved and forgiven me more times than I can count, and so many more than I deserve. I thank Jesus for giving me the strength to tell these stories and for His grace in allowing me to survive them.

**I THANK HIM FOR FINDING ME
WORTH DYING FOR.**

I also dedicate this book to my loving wife, Robbye, who has stood by me through the most challenging events mentioned in these pages—and has loved me through it all. I thank her for helping me keep the story in chronological order, as I found it difficult to recall the timeline of some of the most challenging moments in my life. Mostly, though, thank you for leading me back to Him.

To my children, Joshua, Meghan, Matthew, and Selby—I dedicate this book to you for the sacrifices you've made by having a father whose career choice takes him away so much—both physically and emotionally. I love you all and hope that all who read these words know that you have my heart, my love, my dedication, and my sincerest apologies for the pain I may have caused you. My greatest hope for you is that you find your hope in Jesus and that you follow Him to find the joy that it took me so very long to find.

To my mother, Linda, and my father, Jim, who raised me with the courage of conviction and an example of love for others. Thank you for teaching me the things I needed to know to eventually stand in the light that I have truly only recently found.

To Pastor Joe Champion for his guidance—both with this work and in my life.

To Pastor Ken DeHart, who read my first manuscript for this book and offered his insight, wisdom, and guidance.

To so many pastors and fellow members of Celebration Church in Georgetown, Texas, for welcoming this prodigal home.

To my fellow trial lawyers: warriors for justice, I dedicate this work to the struggle you embrace and suffer daily for clients you sacrifice so much to a public who scorns your existence.

Finally, to the people of this world who fight the good fight, stand up against the Goliath's in their day and do it, armed only in the strength of Lord Jesus Christ.

And to you—yes, you—whom I've not had the privilege yet to meet. Thank you for taking the time to read my story. I am truly honored that you would spend some of your valuable life reading about my own. Your support means the world to me, and I'd love to invite you to join me on the rest of this journey. Please invite everyone you know to join the cause of spreading God's hope and light to those who cannot continue to face the weight of their own life's journey alone. Together, we can lead others to the light that can save them.

To each of you, I ask that you gift yourself the goal of living each day in the fullness of God's love as best as you can—no matter what pain or hardships may plague your seconds, minutes, hours, or even days. Know that no matter how dark or complex the challenge—however unlikely or impossible a better tomorrow may seem—you can rise above it! We are not defeated by saying, "no" to what hurts us and calling out to God for help. Instead, like the mythical, mystical, majestic Phoenix, only then can we pull ourselves out of the ashes, transformed—reborn—finally able to fly free in the love of Jesus Christ! If you or someone you know is ever stuck in the dark or needs assistance, please don't hesitate to contact me or to reach out to a professional for help. Finally, your online review of this book would be greatly appreciated.

Thank you!

Love, Todd

> WALK IN A MANNER WORTHY OF THE LORD, TO PLEASE HIM IN ALL RESPECTS, BEARING FRUIT IN EVERY GOOD WORK AND INCREASING IN THE KNOWLEDGE OF GOD.
>
> —— COLOSSIANS 1:10 ——

CONTENTS

- ADVANCE PRAISES iii
- FOREWORD XIII
- INTRODUCTION XVII
- WHEN EGO ENDS IT ALL 2
- IN UNDER .05 SECONDS 10
- FREEDOM OR FAILURE 18
- GIVING IT ALL TO LOSE EVERYTHING 26
- FATHERS, FOOD, AND FAILURES 32
- YOU CAN'T BEAT BIOLOGY (ALONE) 40
- THE ILLUSION OF PURPOSE AND PERFECTION 50
- JULY 10, 1987, QUANTICO, VIRGINIA. 52
- ABOUT DAMNED TIME 58
- BE CAREFUL WHAT YOU PRAY FOR 68
- BREAKUPS, BREAKDOWNS, AND BREAKTHROUGHS 72
- FAILURE TO EVOLVE 80
- THE #1 RULE OF DEATH PENALTY SCHOOL 90
- REALITY SUCKS 96
- WHEN THE TRUTH CAN NO LONGER BE DENIED 104
- OUT OF THE FRYING PAN AND INTO THE FIRE 110
- THE RETURN OF THE PATRIOT 118
- THE MORALITY OF MONEY 124
- CHILD-LIKE STUBBORNNESS 134
- COLD NIGHTS AND TEXAS CHARM 140
- THE ABANDONMENT OF OUR LIBERTIES 146
- THE TOXIC AMERICAN DREAM 154
- SIN MULTIPLIED 158
- FROM ONE ADDICTION TO ANOTHER 164
- RACING INTO THE BRICK WALL 170
- THE TRUE HEART OF A (GOOD) TRIAL LAWYER . 178

SECRETS, SEX, AND LOTS OF SUCCESS (OR SO I THOUGHT)	184
THE DIRTY LITTLE SECRETS ABOUT MILITARY CONTRACTORS	190
YOU CAN'T OUTRUN THE DEVIL	200
RIDE OR DIE	208
RETROSPECTION, REASON, AND THE REAL WORLD	220
WHEN LIFE ROCKS YOU TO THE CORE	226
BUT GOD	232
THEY NEED YOU	236
LEADERS EAT LAST	242
THE REALITY OF SUCCESS	250
THE PHOENIX ALWAYS RISES	256
THE FEAR OF REPEATING DEFEAT	262
DIE TO SELF —LIVE FOR GOD	268
GOD ALWAYS WINS	276
THE TRUTH ABOUT SUICIDE	282
GOD IS NEVER LATE	290
THE HEART OF FATHERS	298
ABOUT THE AUTHOR	307

FOREWORD

ASHES TO ASHES. Dust to dust. The hostage of Baghdad endured unspeakable horrors, but a phoenix arose to help vulnerable women subjected to the most egregious violations. Over a six-year period, the phoenix died under flames of combustion, decomposed, and was born again to shoulder the battle and pains offer to women suffering similar atrocities.

I was nicknamed the "Hostage of Baghdad," a title that no one would envy.

> *"In the deserts of Iraq, a war is going on against the enemies of America. In the heat and dust of the summer of 2005, a young American went to fight, not against Al-Qaeda, but for her own survival. She became the "Hostage of Baghdad," held against her will by villains of the desert, thousands of miles away from home in Texas."*
> ~ *Congressman Ted Poe, 2007*

Worth Dying For
L. Todd Kelly

When I decided to speak out against the atrocities I experienced in Iraq, I crossed paths with L. Todd Kelly. Broken and afraid, I found an advocate who became my trial lawyer. An attorney who was fiercely compassionate and could internalize my wounds and trauma, he understood my yearning to raise national awareness of the plight of American contractors who were victimized while working abroad for government contractors.

All I wanted was for no other woman: wife, daughter, or friend to experience the nightmare I called my life. L. Todd Kelly became my sword and shield.

HE PUT UP A BIG FIGHT THAT HE FELT WAS WORTH DYING FOR.

Arm in arm, we watched laws passed in my honor; he helped me slay the corporate dragons. But ultimately, Goliath proved to be too big of an opponent. With stocks plummeting and bad press, the enemy was thirsty for blood and continued to victimize and try to turn us into pariahs in the media. With devastation greater than what we could mentally conceptualize, it was hard to envision a real future. Todd couldn't bear knowing the savage battle that I survived in Iraq, the miscarriage of justice in the courtroom, and the subsequent rape in the media.

Sometimes problems are more significant than what we can handle ourselves. As my protector, it shattered Todd as it shattered me. However, even after losing the trial, his blood, sweat, and tears gave me

Worth Dying For
L. Todd Kelly

closure by helping me make the world a better place for future generations of women. Little did he know, he was, and will always be, my hero.

~ Jamie Leigh Jones

Worth Dying For
L. Todd Kelly

INTRODUCTION

WHY IN THE world would anyone want to read my book? While I can't answer that question directly, I initially wrote *Worth Dying For to influence or impact* two groups of people: Professionals who deal with secondary stress and everyone else—who may unknowingly enhance or be impacted by that stress.

TO THOSE WHO DIRECTLY DEAL WITH SECONDARY STRESS:

First Responders, Military, Attorneys, Clergy—must often suffer in excruciating silence. These dedicated service people cannot show signs of weakness—diminishing the ability to generate confidence before a public where professionals compete for clients and struggle to keep a positive public appearance. As an attorney, my clients need someone strong and confident to fight for them when they've been hurt.

Worth Dying For
L. Todd Kelly

They now face a well-funded opponent who prepared for this fight before they ever caused harm; they need someone who is willing to fight a war of attrition to force people to accept less for their, often tragic, devastating losses.

Many professionals remain quiet in this suffering to project an image of strength and confidence. This often puts the problem into a pressure cooker, which causes that burden to intensify until the desperation to alleviate it results in extreme reactions such as bouts of drunkenness, drug abuse, and suicide, which are all too familiar in some professions.

IS THIS CAUSE ONE WORTH DYING FOR?

I write to you, my fellow sufferers, so that you know that you are not alone and understand that you don't have to let the pressure build that way. There can be strength in admitting your weaknesses.

TO THE PUBLIC:

Sometimes, without any intent to cause harm, indifference, and occasional disdain to this problem can intensify these feelings in the very professionals you may need one day to call on for help.

With regard to my own legal profession, I've come to understand that many people hate attorneys because corporations, particularly insurance companies, have told the public to hate us. These

Worth Dying For
L. Todd Kelly

corporate entities have created a public narrative of evil and greed. Rather than focus on the fact that these protector professions are the ones who hold those entities accountable when their very actions harm individuals—corporations and lobbying groups spend a lot of money to convince the public that we are the problem, and they have done it well.

They have done it for so long that their self-serving rhetoric is accepted as truth, regardless of whether any factual background supports it. It always shocks me when a family member of one of these entities asks me to help them. Really! Against the wall you built?

A few of our fellow professional sisters and brothers who advertise in front of their jet planes or other symbols of opulence have fueled this image of greed. These few *bad apples* have damaged the reputation by fostering a false narrative, considering that most attorneys do not live in affluence; most of us carry mortgages on modest homes, pay student loans, and make payments on average cars.

These *bad apples* are a disservice to the rest who must stand before people like you and talk. Ego, here, has damaged our professions. But the public doesn't realize those driven by ego do not represent the majority of attorneys. Most of us are truly good people just trying to make a living by helping others whose lives have suffered because of the actions of another.

There is a financial motive behind making you hate us. Follow the money. Who do you suppose benefits if you think less of us or believe that we are out to harm vs. help you?

Worth Dying For
L. Todd Kelly

As to certain other professionals, there is always a motive behind those who would denigrate the very purpose of the profession.

Who is telling the world that as a group the police are bad? Who says the same thing of clergy? In each instance there are examples of those who would shame us, but are these professions as a group bad? Of course not, and that is the point.

> WHEN WE, AS A SOCIETY, GROUP EVERY PERSON OF ANY CLASS OF PEOPLE INTO ONE CATEGORY, WE MISS THE TRUTH.

It is in these struggles that many of us, who are dedicated to the service of others, lose ourselves. We become caught in a battle that many will, quite literally, die for. This dedication is a battle that almost killed me and shaped the trajectory of my own life. That is why I must ask:

IS IT WORTH DYING FOR?

WORTH DYING FOR

SACRIFICE, SUCCESS, AND SUBMITTING TO LIFE'S GREATEST TRUTH

WHEN EGO ENDS IT ALL

Ego

My ego is too large, you say.
I now think that you're right.
My belief that it had been destroyed
Could not explain my plight.

If your assessment were untrue
Then your words would have no might.
And every time you put me down
I wouldn't feel the slight.

You've made me reassess my view
Of who I truly am.
And though it clearly evades you
My confidence is sham.

Ego, yes, I have one still
Despite its beaten, ragged, shell.
And judge me, oh I know you will—
But you have not lived in my Hell.

So, when you call me out next time
For all the world to see—
This low-life piece of filthy slime,
You hurt the friend in me.
I came to you a broken man
Whose ego suffered most.
Before I lost it by my hand
I was far too quick to boast.

I boasted of success and fame
And all the things I'd done.
For I knew how to play this game
But had forgot the One.

Perhaps that's why your words won't leave:
Why should I even care
If it's to His Love that I cleave?
Perhaps my ego's still in there?

So thanks, I guess, for calling out
This raging flaw in me.
And making sure it really hurt
So everyone can see.

The truth has reared its nasty head:
Ego's not gone, it seems.
Whether working late or froze in dread,
It made nightmares out of dreams.

• • • • • • • • • • • • •

Worth Dying For
L. Todd Kelly

**LATE JUNE 2011,
RICHMOND, TEXAS.**

THEY'RE GONE...THE WOMAN I have betrayed so many times during our twenty-year marriage has taken our daughter, Meghan, shopping. That's what they do when she comes home from college—spend money I can't keep up with.

The boys, too, are out for the day. My sons, Josh and Matthew, love to visit with their friends. They are probably killing aliens or sharpenin their skills on the latest version of *World of Warcraft.*

Thank God they aren't home. If they could see the effect that these demons in my head have had on their father today...

The scent of single malt Scotch comes in wafts, together with the bad breath of a man who hasn't eaten in days.

I'm in my *dream home*—the one I built to die in. I awake in the same reclining chair I have been in for three days. I've been lifelessly existing in this recliner in front of the noisy screen across the room, mercilessly playing news recounts of the events that put me here.

I have not shaved or bathed since I took off my suit three days ago. I stink of body odor and whatever food I have spilled on myself. I quit drinking when I finished the whiskey bottle at the foot of this recliner. Some of that adds to the pungent aroma of my chosen spot. Perhaps it isn't on the chair, but on the grey terry cloth bathrobe that has adorned my beaten frame for the

Worth Dying For
L. Todd Kelly

past three days. The very sight of me in this moment would have repulsed me a week ago.

Today, I simply don't care.

I do find the strength to make it to the restroom. Or at least I believe I do because that aroma isn't sharing this chair with me. But as soon as I can, I return to the chair, stare at the TV, and wallow—just as I have for the past three days.

Then, there's the debt. The Stillwater Asset-Backed Fund has sued me for the $12 Million they say I owe them. This is more than I could ever repay. I am financially ruined.

I know I should go to work. I can't face the people there. They were so hopeful for me. I was so sure I would win. I failed.

This is what failure looks like.

My thoughts occasionally drift to the only thing outside of my children that has me questioning the inevitable end to this misery: Robbye. I wonder where she is. She stayed away from the trial that she had worked so hard on to avoid a scene with Marysue. That would have been an even greater disaster. I hope she's okay.

I should call her. I can't. I should tell her that I still love her. I can't bring myself to talk to another person. After all, I let her down, too.

I convene in the sitting area in the bedroom I share with Marysue, which now serves as my sanctuary,

Worth Dying For
L. Todd Kelly

unaware that the demons in my head would soon come to offer me an escape from the misery I created.

I should call Robbye. I can't. Things will be better for her this way. Any minute now and the demon's presence will be inescapable…

It will be better for everyone if I make this quick. The pain of delaying this decision will only make it worse for everyone who has ever cared about me. It will make it worse for me.

However badly I don't want anyone—especially Meghan, Joshua, or Matthew, to feel the pain of my departure—they'll be better off for it. They realize there's no escape from the burden of my past mistakes, and they'll move on knowing I had done everything I could to teach them that.

Most importantly, they'll learn never to make the same mistakes I have, which opened the door to the minions who won't stop gnawing at my soul.

I shake my head, battling the pain. I can't keep stalling lest I draw their attention to my balking. But the movie keeps rewinding and looping in my mind all the same. News of my trial loss is all over the major network news sources: CNN, NBC, Fox News, ABC, The New York Times, The Wall Street Journal…and every other carnivorous syndicate known to the North American continent.

It's not just my name and my law firm's reputation that's been impugned. Jamie, the courageous woman I fought so hard for, and all of the women that she stood for by coming forward with her case—all of the women

Worth Dying For
L. Todd Kelly

I was fighting so hard to protect in this public battle—no longer have a name and the sense of justice they deserve because of me, my pride, and my foolishness...or at least what I've now come to feel is foolishness.

I feel their SORROW. *Every ounce of it.*

I feel their PAIN. *Every minute of it.*

I feel their SUFFERING. *Its entire weight bearing down on my shoulders.*

I, alone, am responsible for the continuation of this pain...

To say that I failed myself, these women, and everyone around me would be a complete and total understatement. This loss was no superficial one. I had failed in a deep, penetrating level known only to those who risk everything for what they believe in and come up short. I have failed as a lawyer, as a husband, as a father, as a friend, as a man, and as a child of God.

Speaking of God, I ignored Him for so long that I am sure He is no longer around for me. I probably should get up and put an end to this pain before I am denied any chance of sanctuary from this dark, inescapable pit.

The time, I think, *has come.*

Worth Dying For
L. Todd Kelly

FATHER'S LOVE. A Father's Love requires sacrifice. We need to focus on which sacrifices are good and life-bringing, versus those that are life-ending and encouraged by demonic forces that serve only to harm.

FATHER'S LIFE. A Father's Life is precious—but not only to him. Our lives are precious to our children and families, just as our Heavenly Father's life was precious to Him and to each of us when he sacrificed it out of his love for us.

FATHER'S FEAR. A Father Fears that he will fail his family. This can be wrapped up in emotional, financial, and physical failures. Satan will lie to a father, saying, you have failed, as he preys upon these earthly fears. There is an answer to this lie.

FATHER'S FIGHT. A Father's Fight is for his children. He must fight to protect them from outside forces, but what does a father do when the demons confronting his children are coming from him?

FATHER'S WISDOM: A Father's Wisdom should lead his children to walk away from their ego and walk to the foot of the cross.

Worth Dying For
L. Todd Kelly

IN UNDER .05 SECONDS

2

The Friend

The cold impersonal,
deadly feel,
The instrument of
polished steel.
How could it ever be a
friend
When it's very purpose
was to end?

To end the lives that it
confronted,
To end the hunter—as
the hunted.
Its' purpose death—that
much is clear.
No wonder owning it
caused fear.

Oh, you may even become
fond,
And with it you may, with
others, bond,
But it has only one true
goal,
To leave a bloody, deadly
hole.

So, fear this weapon, and
all it does
It will destroy all your life
was.
Not just the bad, but the
good, too.
Trust it, and it's the last
you'll do.

· · · · · ● ● ● · · · ·

ALONE IN THIS HOUSE, I crawl across my bedroom floor and gather myself in a cross-legged heap on the floor of my walk-in master bedroom closet. My eyes fix on the object of my desire: a light green pistol bag with leather handles. The light tan carpet Marysue selected for this *dream home* proves to be comfortable enough.

I sit…amidst the array of black, grey, and blue business suits, hanging above the western shirts and starched blue jeans hung meticulously in front of me. My side of the closet is a throwback to a wall locker ready for inspection during Basic School at Quantico.

Worth Dying For
L. Todd Kelly

My attention returns to the demonic noises in my head.

"Just open the damned thing, Todd!
Do it now! Do it quickly and get it over with!
End your pain!"

The 9mm Beretta M9 pistol sits within my reach, safely stored in its holster, inside my range bag. I know there are ten hollow point rounds of ammo in the magazine, which were created to do one thing—kill a man. The magazine is sitting loosely in the handle, not locked in place. I don't want to take the chance that a through-and-through will leave my family burdened with an invalid.

Despite my training as a Marine, I have never wanted to have firearms in the house where my children play—or where they sneak in at night after being out too late. The thought of standing over the lifeless body of a teenager who snuck in late at night unannounced, holding a pistol that was still smoking from the barrel, absolutely terrified me. Whether it's my own child or one of their friends, that is more guilt than I could ever face. The slight chance of a burglar is just not worth a child dying for. Perhaps this inevitable moment in the closet is another reason I never consciously considered it until now.

One quick squeeze and the pain will end.

Just a few weeks ago, I soaked in the adulation of those watching me wage this battle. Now fallen, those fair-weather-friends are quick to ridicule the last ounce of pride I hold on to for sustenance.

Worth Dying For
L. Todd Kelly

How easily people can turn on each other.

THE EMBARRASSMENT WILL BE OVER. No one will be mocking me—at least not that I will be aware of. I will be dead. I am so embarrassed to have fallen this far from the man I intended to be!

THE SHAME—GONE—AT LEAST FOR ME. My shame in having taken these roads is more than I can bear. I used to see myself as the *good guy*. I don't even know that person now. My shame will die with me. But who will carry it after I am gone?

Those who watched my life unravel so publicly will probably believe that I found my most recent trial loss too much to take.

> **I ALSO HAD TO ADDRESS THAT MY SHAME IN LOSING SO PUBLICLY WAS WORTH DYING FOR.**

It's a pretty pistol, I think to myself. *I have maintained it meticulously.*

"Take it out," the demons scream in my head!

In obedience to the demons' demands, I take it out of the bag and draw it from the black canvas shoulder holster where it rests. It smells of CLR and carbon, remnants of lessons learned as a Marine—I take care of my weapons. I take in that smell as if it were a familiar friend, one that I once knew I could depend upon to save my life if that moment ever came. A friend who

Worth Dying For
L. Todd Kelly

had never failed me—never betrayed me. This weapon has always fit so well in my hand.

I have become all too comfortable with her curves.

The Beretta M9 is the only pistol I felt comfortable purchasing when my son, Josh, announced, at 21 years of age, that he would purchase a pistol and asked his Marine Veteran father to help him choose which one he should buy. The first part of his statement was not a question, so I agreed to his request for help and found my pistol on the trip to the sporting goods store.

I bought this nine with the thought that shooting would be something I could do with Josh—to teach him since I had never allowed firearms in the house when he was young. The oft-feared image of that dead child had been strong and vivid.

THE COMFORT THAT THE PROTECTION A FIREARM AFFORDS HAS SIMPLY NEVER BEEN WORTH A CHILD DYING FOR.

She makes it a point to remind me of our first date, at the range, with my sons. I have surely had some quality time with Josh and Matthew at the range. Meghan, too—though it's not her thing.

Josh loves it, and I think Matthew loves to be part of the outings. I can see Josh holding his own 9mm weapon down range as I hover over him, teaching him about sight alignment and sight picture. I recall the pride of both boys as they pulled back their first targets

Worth Dying For
L. Todd Kelly

with shots in the kill zone of those life-sized paper bad guys.

Those photographs were treasures.
Those memories, even more so.
We also liked to shoot my old British 303, but it was a difficult rifle to master.

I release the magazine to check the load. Yep, ten of the hollow points are still in there so as not to tax the spring in the magazine too much. I slide the magazine home: locked and loaded. My weapon stands ready for a home invader, nervous misses and all. It only takes one of these to protect a home—or end a life.

I am well-trained on this one. "Squeeze. Don't Pull." I hear my weapons instructor's voice echo, recalling my time in the Corps.

We were taught how to squeeze the trigger and how to reload fast. I guess that the second part now proves irrelevant.

I can almost use this one in my sleep—a natural part of the fear and the image that prevented her purchase for so long.

My *right* to own a weapon was simply not worth a child dying for.

Worth Dying For
L. Todd Kelly

FATHER'S LOVE. A Father's Love often encourages him to teach children to protect themselves from danger.

FATHER'S LIFE. A Father's Life should be lived to exemplify strength and courage to his children.

FATHER'S FEAR. A Father Fears that some harm may come to his family—especially a harm that he believes he can prevent.

FATHER'S FIGHT. A Father's Fight is to ensure that his children are well protected without instilling deadly habits in them.

FATHER'S WISDOM. A Father's Wisdom should lead his children to do what is good and right in the eyes of God.

Worth Dying For
L. Todd Kelly

FREEDOM OR FAILURE

3

Special

I thought that I was special then,
Somehow stronger than other men.
But looking now it's little more,
Than my ego shattered on the floor.

The enemy I thought I could defeat
Has left me knocked down off my feet.
But now I've lost more than a case,
That's more than egg upon my face.

I've been free to chase my selfish dreams,
But freedom has a price, it seems.

My life must be worth some amount,
Or did it ever even count?

I've freely chased every selfish want,
But it was God I seemed to taunt.
What a fool I was to turn,
In Hell I now deserve to burn.

My death is just one squeeze away,
Why should I live another day?
I've done so much to turn from Him
That's why my life has grown so dim.

•••••••••••

I HALF SMILE IMAGINING the pain, embarrassment, and shame immediately disappearing in a puff of smoke.

All of the guilt—gone! All of the suffering—relieved!

I can already imagine the looks of those who've judged me when they learn about what happened to me. Just a cliché. I place my weapon of choice into my mouth. The demonic voices engage, in soothing, almost maternal tones.

Worth Dying For
L. Todd Kelly

Will anyone even care?

Won't this be better?

You're insured for more than you're worth, anyway!

Trial Lawyers do this all the time—You'll just be another sad statistic. Right?

Your family could use the money. God knows you haven't been able to provide it.

Why did I think I was so special? Why did I think that the world's largest military contractor couldn't find a way to beat me? Even if I knew deep down that they would spare no expense and try it without scruples?

Why do I care so much?

"Are you there, God?"

I try to interrupt...the demonic tones change:

He's not listening to you, Todd. You turned your back on Him years ago. Why do you call upon Him now?

Just pull the damned trigger. End it.

You are a terrible lawyer! You are all hype.

The whole world just watched you publicly eat it against Halliburton's lawyers. Who's laughing now!?

You knew they were better than you the whole time!

You know she was raped. You know what they did to her...and you just let them get away with it.

Worth Dying For
L. Todd Kelly

Now everyone sees you for what you are. FRAUD! You just aren't that Good!

Your marriage is a fraud, too. Your wife doesn't trust you—you've betrayed her too many times to count. All you're good for now is what you can bring home to her. And now, you can't bring home a damned thing.

You are, quite literally, worth more dead.

Your kids are embarrassed by you; even their friends know what you are.

You spend too much time at work, the dojo, or anywhere but home.

You're a cheater. Everyone knows you've been unfaithful to your wife!

Your parents are so ashamed of you! They used to be so proud.

You are a failure. Pull the trigger!

A deep shiver of fear moves within me as if a hand, frigid, cold, yet invisible presses through my shoulder and forces my muscles to engage, clenching the pistol grip and trigger, nearly engaging the firing pin.

No, that is an eternal sentence in Hell! I plead as I try to remember my Savior.

"What about Robbye?" I almost beg.

There is no way you can ever be with her. Too many obstacles. You will just be miserable if you can't be with her anyway, right?! How can you go on without her in your life now?

Worth Dying For
L. Todd Kelly

Did you learn anything at the ranch? Reverse roles.

How will Joshua and Matthew feel when they find me? Who's gonna clean up the mess that a hollow point will make of my brain? Will that image haunt their memories?

Hell, you don't even remember Lannie, and you have wondered about his death your whole life!

You bear his name—perhaps this is just hereditary.

What kind of an example is this for Meghan? I told her never to quit. Now look what she'll see: QUITTER!

What will this do to the kids who know me–who might still love me?

I am gaining resolve.

"Perhaps they love you. They do not respect you! You will fail your own daughter just like you did those other girls!"

The demons retort!

Leadership—by example! Is this the example I want my children to Emulate?

Leadership? YOU JUST FAILED, MARINE!

You failed EVERY RAPE VICTIM that you thought you could help! You have done more harm than good! Be a man—pull the trigger! They urge.

No! I have to be a man and face my mess.

I cry.

Worth Dying For
L. Todd Kelly

"But what about Robbye?"

"Another woman?"

The demons mock.

"You know you'll only hurt her like you've done your wife and every other woman you've wooed. Do her a favor and pull the damned trigger, Todd! End this all now!"

The demands are more urgent.

The weight of many demons, as invisible as they may be, now completely crushing down on my shoulders. *"Pull the trigger, Todd. Pull it now!"*

My mind races frantically as unbearable pressure and heat engulf my whole body.

My finger, trembling, closes itself tighter on the trigger…

The fight rages inside my head for about forty-five agonizing minutes.

Then, I close my eyes and tell myself,…

MY SINS ARE WORTH DYING FOR.

Worth Dying For
L. Todd Kelly

FATHER'S LOVE. A Father's Love, when it fails to follow the Lord's call, is not enough to set an example that we want our children to follow.

FATHER'S LIFE. A Father's Life should be dedicated to that role, always remembering the example that he sets.

FATHER'S FEAR. A Father's Fear should focus on the harm he can do to his children when he turns from God.

FATHER'S FIGHT. A Father's Fight for life, and to set an example in a world full of distractions, is difficult and one we cannot hope to win without him.

FATHER'S WISDOM. A Father's Wisdom is not enough without the Father's Wisdom.

Worth Dying For
L. Todd Kelly

GIVING IT ALL TO LOSE EVERYTHING

— 4 —

Broken

*Broken homes and
broken spirit,
I knew but didn't want
to hear it.
The way to mend the
hearts unseen.
The pain they cause,
acute and keen.*

*I painted a rosy picture
of
A house shrouded in
human love.
I failed to open up my
heart
To the only One who
could even start*

*To heal the brokenness
inside.
But I was happy. No, I
lied.
I was less than
malcontent.
I forgot that love was
Heaven sent.*

*I didn't have to be alone,
If only I would just
atone.
Admit my sin, accept the
gift
Instead, alone I sit, adrift*

・・・・・●●●・・・・・

THIS HOUSE WAS THE culmination of the dreams forged between my wife, Marysue, and me back when I was still in the Marine Corps and the kids were still riding bikes with training wheels. Well, two of them were—Matthew was still in diapers. We had dreamt of a life in this home and had placed our hope in this physical space, that in the end, simply did not hold.

Marysue had changed. I had too. Certainly, my changed behavior of multiple indiscretions led to the changes in how she treated me. Perhaps the opposite was also true. Perhaps it was a combination. Neither of us addressed the cause and effect of where we had fallen in such a way as to have a firm handle on the answer to that question. What was certain was that I grew to be miserable in the marriage.

Worth Dying For
L. Todd Kelly

My kids, however, were another story. I adored them. Always had. Marysue did, too. She was a good mother to them, and I was as good a father as possible...given that I lived a *secret* life. But I always loved them more than I loved my own life. Marysue had that to hold over me too. How many times did she have to remind me that she never cheated? I knew!

The twins, Joshua and Meghan, were truly miracle babies. They had been born at twenty-seven weeks gestation, weighing less than two pounds each. Marysue and I spent several months in the NICU at Kapiolani Medical Center in Honolulu, Hawaii, praying for their lives. I recall holding these two small children and thinking they were the most beautiful things I had ever seen. For the first time, I understood a father's love for his children.

A LOVE THAT WAS WORTH VIRTUALLY ANY SACRIFICE.

I knew I would have freely given my life to save theirs. I made that offer in prayer often in those first difficult months.

Their early lives, after the twins got out of that scary place, had been spent in and out of medical appointments and eating whatever we could get them actually to take. We just needed them to grow, and we were not above feeding them candy, pizza, cake, ice cream, or anything else that would add caloric intake.

But as I sat in my misery at home in Richmond, they were both in college. Both had graduated high school with high grades, and both were athletic.

Worth Dying For
L. Todd Kelly

Meghan—a high school and competitive cheerleader. Josh—a black belt in Zen Do-Kai Karate.

Matthew had been born early, too—all of three weeks. His birth weight, a whopping six pounds, five ounces, earned him the moniker "Chunk." That would wear off quickly, as he was thin and fit as a kid. Although he started karate with his brother and me, he had a love for soccer that took him out of the dojo. Matthew was quiet and focused on video games. I could barely get him out of the house unless it were to ride in his golf cart (made to look like an all-terrain tactical vehicle) and shoot airsoft guns at his brother and a few friends.

These kids were the reason I kept coming home. They were the driving force behind me to this point. They were the reason I kept pushing on. There had never been any doubt that I loved them. I had been strict with them and occasionally short-tempered, but my love was without question. They looked up to me—or I believed they did before the affairs. But once they knew the truth about those...

Marysue had been kind to me during my miserable days after the Jones trial. She brought me an occasional cup of coffee and whatever food she had prepared for the kids to keep me alive when I didn't want to eat. She offered to sit with me, but I didn't want that. I didn't want anything except to replay the trial that I *should have won* over and over again. That, and I wanted out of the life I once thought I wanted. I wished that she wasn't being kind. I didn't want to be with her anymore. I had thought she understood that. Thoughts ravaged my mind, *why does she hang on? I don't want to be cruel to her, but I don't want this marriage!*

My kids, as kids do, were enjoying their summer off. Josh and Meghan were both home from college. Meghan spent most of her time with her high school best friend, Katelyn. Josh and Matthew were usually upstairs playing one video game or another, which I had always been too busy to learn how to play with them.

Thank God they had each other. I hated those games, but at least they gave the boys a connection. I always wished they would spend some time outside—maybe throw a damned baseball! I knew I should have gotten up to go be with them more often —that they wouldn't be home forever. I just couldn't. I could barely look at them, knowing they didn't feel the same about me anymore. Despite it all, I was—alone.

WAS THIS SELF-INFLICTED PREDICAMENT WORTH DYING FOR?

Worth Dying For
L. Todd Kelly

FATHER'S LOVE. A Father's Love begins before their child is born and is deeper than most relationships he will ever experience. It is sacrificial and deep.

FATHER'S LIFE. A Father's Life is no longer about himself but about his children and his family—when he is doing it right.

FATHER'S FEAR. A Father's Fear for the life of his children can be more powerful than other temptations and desires.

FATHER'S FIGHT. A Father's Fight is to raise his children to be productive members of society. For the Christian father, it is to live a life that honors God.

FATHER'S WISDOM. A Father's Wisdom is an important, but not all-inclusive, guide for his children.

FATHERS, FOOD, AND FAILURES

5

THE FATHER'S LOVE

His son, I learned so much from Dad,
As I grew up, it must have made him sad,
He taught me truth was the mark of a man
I follow his lead the best I can.

He also taught of a family's love,
Not from our blood, but from God above,
He taught me how to love a wife,
As I watched him throughout my life.

The doubts that sometimes came to mind,
Through love have been left far behind.
His love was pure, but he didn't seem
To understand he'd made a dream.

Though he didn't go, he wouldn't stop
And God allowed his word to drop
Into my life as if by chance,
But with the Lord, no happenstance.

My dad protected me from much
And opened doors to allow God's touch.
You need to know I love you, Dad.
But turn to God, or I'll be sad.

For He's my father, and yours, too.
And no matter what else, in love, you do,
Without His love we are lost to sin.
Give Him everything you've been.

•••••••••••

I'M THE OLDEST OF two boys, raised in a loving home by my biological mother and the only father I've ever known. Some would refer to Jim Kelly as my *stepfather* or *adoptive father*. That has never been his role. He was my daddy —until I became too *adult* to call him that in public. Now, he's my dad unless we're alone.

Worth Dying For
L. Todd Kelly

My dad is a man of unyielding integrity, who taught my brother and me that honesty is not the *best policy* but rather the only one. He was born to a poor family just outside of Houston, Texas, and was able to build himself up to become a small business owner in the computer technology field by first joining the Navy and by applying himself aggressively to each job he took thereafter. He demonstrated work ethic and dedication. More than anything else, my dad has shown us what loyalty to family looks like. His love for my mother is still a shining example that all should strive for in marriage.

Similarly, though biologically Jim Kelly's son, Reagan has never been my *half-brother*. He is simply my brother (or *my little sister* when I am teasing him—as we do).

Reagan is four years younger than I am and grew up with me watching over him—not that he needed it. As we have aged, however, we have simply become friends and brothers. He has now had my back as many times as I have his.

My mother, Linda, is a strong figure who taught Reagan and me at an early age about the strength of women while remaining gentle in her love toward us. Though she gave birth to me at the age of 16, her wisdom was always far beyond her tender years, and she has been a constant pillar of strength in our family. Along with my dad, she taught us the value of family and let us draw strength from the stability of the love that we share. She managed the "Precious Jewels" departments of a number of high-end stores until she

Worth Dying For
L. Todd Kelly

retired from Neiman Marcus after years of dedicated service.

I OFTEN REFLECT ON HOW THANKFUL I AM THAT SHE WAS MY MOTHER AND NOT MY BOSS.

Lannie Ross Cross was my biological father. I was barely a year old when he died, so I have no memory of him. Jim Kelly is truly my dad. Two competing stories surround Lannie Cross' death. He was either killed by local police officers connected to organized crime after they beat him too badly for mouthing off, or he killed himself by hanging. These stories are equally convincing from family members I love and trust. I wonder about what truly took his life. That curiosity would echo in the recesses of my mind and rear its head periodically throughout my life.

My grandparents, Jewel Cross and Jethro Cross (Lannie's parents) were Christians who instilled in me a curiosity about Jesus early on during my annual two-week summer vacations with them in Camden, Arkansas. These were simple, God-loving people who loved me unconditionally—if not exceptionally—as I seemed to serve as a stand-in for their son, who died too young, even though they had eight other living children. This special love stayed with me until they died in 1989. Though I have no memory of Lannie Cross at all, what I know of him is through the stories that they would tell me around a table filled with iced

Worth Dying For
L. Todd Kelly

tea, dominoes, and a palpable love for God and family virtually every night that I spent with them.

Several of my relatives on the Cross side were (and are) pastors, including an uncle and a first cousin. I was always awed by that connection with our Heavenly Father but never felt that particular call on my life.

My dad (Jim) worked for Bell Helicopter International during the reign of Shah Reza Pahlavi while I was in elementary school. Mid-way through my fourth-grade year, my family arrived in Isfahan, Iran, where I spent four of my formative years in a community with Persian neighbors. I did not return home to my native Texas until halfway through the eighth grade.

This childhood experience in a third-world country provided me with an appreciation of the United States at a very early age. The simple freedoms we take for granted were not present, even in pre-Ayatollah Iran. Women walked behind their husbands to show their *place* in society. Their faces and heads were covered with *chadors* so as not to *tempt other men*. Food was different, to say the least. Dairy was not as well pasteurized, and I had to learn to appreciate cream at the top of the milk bottle. My parents boiled our drinking water before we drank it to avoid diseases that our American bodies were not immune to. Peanut butter came from a blender of fresh peanuts—not a jar of Jif®. Snickers® candy—that was a rare treat, indeed.

The American School of Isfahan was attended by an eclectic group of kids from all over the United States as well as other ex-patriots and even a few Iranian

Worth Dying For
L. Todd Kelly

children who were born to the wealthy, connected group of military leaders and royalty in this third-world nation. They all spoke English well enough to attend. These people, while they practiced a different religion from most that I know, were very warm and inviting—they were my introduction to Islam.

It was during a summer in Iran, while my parents were vacationing in Greece, that some family friends took Reagan and me to a makeshift church that had been planted in our elementary school cafeteria. The school itself was a four-story building, with the classrooms on the upper floors. The cafeteria was clean, with white and gray tiled floors. The *pews* were simply rows of folding chairs that the kids used during lunch hours on weekdays. The altar was about six inches high with plywood flooring. This place was not fancy, but God was there. I felt Him.

Family friends, Howard and June Brook, attended services regularly and took us to church with their family one Sunday. Though I was only a child in the fifth grade, I understood clearly when I heard God's call upon my heart for the first time. I answered my first altar call when the pastor asked if I wanted salvation. I felt His presence as I walked to the front of the church and received Jesus into my heart. I was overwhelmed by His presence in my body.

I was Baptized two weeks later in a church-wide service at one of the rivers flowing into the Caspian Sea, making my love of Christ and

Worth Dying For
L. Todd Kelly

acceptance of Him as my Lord and Savior public for all in attendance that day.

> I LEARNED ABOUT THE SALVATION AVAILABLE TO ALL MANKIND THAT JESUS SOMEHOW, THROUGH A LOVE I STILL CANNOT FULLY UNDERSTAND, FOUND WORTHY OF DYING FOR.

With child-like faith, I understood that Jesus suffered an excruciating and humiliating death that He did not deserve as payment for my sin—before I even committed it. I also knew that:

He was resurrected from death.
He was still alive—I FELT HIM.
He would return—I WAS SAVED.

Mom and Dad did not regularly attend church services, and my education regarding God and Biblical theology was sporadic.

Despite our religious and cultural differences, we generally felt safe in Isfahan until about 1978, when the Shah was overthrown by Ayatollah Khomeini and retreated into exile. My dad knew we had to leave once we started seeing "Yankee Go Home" painted on the side of the houses of fellow Americans. Being from Texas, I recall thinking: *I'm no "Yankee!" I'm from Texas.*

THIS GOOD-PAYING JOB AND STAYING TO SELL OUR BELONGINGS WAS SIMPLY NOT A PRICE WORTH DYING FOR.

Worth Dying For
L. Todd Kelly

FATHER'S LOVE. A Father's Love is nurturing and provides for the growth of his children. This is true of earthly fathers but even more of our Heavenly Father.

FATHER'S LIFE. A Father's Life is dedicated to the enrichment of his children and his family—how much more is the dedication of our Heavenly Father?

FATHER'S FEAR. A Father's Fear for the safety of his children is evident in most attentive fathers. The fear of our failure to seek Him is the fear of our Heavenly Father.

FATHER'S FIGHT. A Father's Fight is to help his children to rise above them (whether in wealth, social status, or favor with God). Which are you doing?

FATHER'S WISDOM: A Father's Wisdom guides this world. What guides us into the next?

YOU CAN'T BEAT BIOLOGY (ALONE)

6

Addicted

As a boy I do not know the harm,
Awaiting just beyond the charm.
We chased the girls and thought it cool,
'Cause that's the talk of boys at school.

Never thinking of harm I'd cause,
Just like a wonder straight from Oz.
Emotions burning without control,
Or concern that I might pay a toll.

Ignoring risk, it just "feels right."
Perhaps another quest tonight?
Perhaps emotion, perhaps just skin,
That last encounter left me thin.

It's like a drug and I, it's slave,
I know it's wrong to thus behave,
But who's the victim? Where's the crime?
Besides, I'm only marking time.

With each new partner, I am less
But I push on— despite the mess.
Those closest to me should distrust,
For I have given in to lust.

I do not want to be this man
But fill a void, I think this can.
So I chase sex as if my next meal,
Momentary highs are all I steal.

•••••••••••

WHEN MY FAMILY RETURNED to my hometown of Arlington, Texas, I was about halfway through the eighth grade. Junior high school kids are harsh, and I had been out of the country (and their lives) for the better part of four years. I had no place in this group. I had to fight my way into acceptance—quite literally. As a *new* kid from a *weird* country with an unfortunately

Worth Dying For
L. Todd Kelly

bad case of acne—at a time before medications were developed well enough to deal with that embarrassment effectively, girls were not exactly beating down my doors, either. This general lack of acceptance by the fairer sex would become a yardstick that I used to measure my self-worth for many years.

This weakness would become Satan's greatest weapon against my soul in my personal struggle to remain faithful to Jesus for much of my life after these formative struggles.

> IF GIRLS GIVE ME ATTENTION, THEN I MUST BE WORTHY.

As girls were not happening in my life, I focused on my Boy Scout progress. I enjoyed the camping and the leadership skills that I was learning. Fortunately, my Scoutmasters were truly good men and not the type that would later give scouting such a bad name by giving in to their own demons and victimizing so many other boys.

I was accepted into an elite group of Scouts called the Order of the Arrow and eventually attained the rank of Eagle Scout. I was proud of these accomplishments as I stood before family and friends to be awarded my Eagle Scout badge at my Eagle Court of Honor.

I played tight end for the James Bowie High School Volunteers, a District 5A football team that won a lot

Worth Dying For
L. Todd Kelly

more than we lost. I actively concealed my involvement with the Boy Scouts of America, however. It was somehow embarrassing in this crowd of athletes whose respect I desperately coveted. The team was great. I was perhaps only slightly above average but did bring a lot of heart to the game—and normally left a lot of blood on the field—my own. Fortunately for my economic future, my grades were much better than my skills on the field, and I would not have to rely upon my prowess under the Friday night lights to make ends meet.

One of my strong suits was writing. Though I didn't know why, I actually enjoyed it. Like my Eagle Scout award, this part of my life was not *cool*, so I hid this attribute from my peers, too. I thought I would like to be an attorney someday. Perry Mason and Matlock television shows and other representations that glorified the profession of law filled my mind with this image of a *noble profession* for someone who wants to help others.

I did manage to attract one girl in high school. Carolyn was my first love, and she did a lot to boost my confidence. What I didn't realize yet was that I was judging my own self-worth on how well she perceived me.

WE BELIEVED, AT THE RIPE OLD AGE OF 16, THAT WE WERE, TO EACH OTHER, WORTH DYING FOR.

Worth Dying For
L. Todd Kelly

One Friday night, I came particularly close to fulfilling that call. Carolyn loved everything cowboy, so naturally, I wanted to show her just how *cowboy* I could be. Sitting atop a two-thousand-pound bull seemed like a great idea from afar. I stretched my toes around the giant animal as far as they could reach. The leather glove on my left hand held tight to the rigging that my friends had cinched down for me to hold on to.

Just eight seconds, Todd, then jump to the side and run. The clowns will take it from there.

I raised my right hand—signaling to the chute operator that I was ready. I wasn't.

As the bull jumped to his left, I followed him for that first move. This instilled in me a fleeting sense of confidence.

I've got this.

When he turned back toward his right—okay, when he whipped back to the right, I quickly discovered that my buddy's skills at cinching down the rigging needed some work. The loose rigging slipped on the mammoth animal as I started to slide off his left side. My grip, born more of fear than athletic ability, kept me connected to the bull—if only loosely.

Now, I'm not sure how many *real* cowboys out there can boast of having completed an eight-second ride on the underside of a bucking bull. I can. It turns out that getting off the ride while trying to dodge the hooves of a bucking bull is quite the challenge—particularly

Worth Dying For
L. Todd Kelly

when you are dangling from underneath the angry animal when you do it.

If I time this just right...
My timing was not right.

The bull's hoof tore into my left abdomen as he dropped down for one more move. The excruciating pain was immediately overcome by fear as the scared animal turned to come back.

The clowns yelled at me, "Run!" They didn't have to yell twice.

Adrenaline is a superpower, and I was able to clear the gate into the stands where Carolyn sat, worried.

Carolyn was somehow impressed by the *manliness* of this event. I accepted her adulation.

The wounds healed. I would do that again for the pay-off, I thought.

Carolyn struggled with English Literature. I was in an honors class during the same class period.

I cannot let her fail.
I would do anything to help her.
Look at what she's done for me.

I dropped my honors English to take English with Carolyn. That way, I would be able to work on the same assignments with her and could tutor her that way. It worked. She did well.

We dated for the rest of high school.

Worth Dying For
L. Todd Kelly

I graduated high school in 1983—20th in a class of 640. I often wonder where I would have ended up if I hadn't dropped that honors English class. I moved to Austin, Texas, to attend the University of Texas. I was still a good student—thankfully because I did what too many freshman students at UT do.

I drank—a lot.

I was not walking in God's will and had almost forgotten that I gave my life to Him.

Sixth Street was my favorite weekend location. My acne was cleared up, and I'd found a long-desired form of entertainment, and perceived self-worth, in the opposite sex. Because I didn't look for fulfillment from God, I received a substitute in the bedroom. But, as it does, that momentary thrill just left me seeking more—the satisfaction served as only a temporary salve on my broken ego.

> AS ANY DRUG ADDICT WILL TELL YOU, THE MOMENTARY HIGH IS TOO ADDICTIVE TO STOP—EVEN WHEN YOU KNOW THE DAMAGE YOU ARE DOING.

I continued to attend worship services on rare occasions, or when I visited my grandparents in Arkansas during the summertime breaks throughout my college years.

In 1985, I met Debbie, a sorority girl who was a couple of years my senior. She introduced herself by

Worth Dying For
L. Todd Kelly

making a sexually explicit comment as she poured me a beer from a keg at a fraternity party, I had no business attending. Well, no legitimate reason anyway, as I was not in the fraternity. Debbie and I started talking. Debbie was a pretty, dark-haired girl who clearly knew how to work in a room full of people. She was generally likable, and sorority trained to carry a conversation. She decided that my boots and western shirts were not the proper look for her significant other to wear. So I changed that without protest. Boat shoes and polo shirts took over my daily wear

---
ANYTHING FOR THE AFFECTION OF A GIRL!

    We had been dating ever since that first meeting at the keg and started talking about *forever*. I was not through with college, so I decided to drop out and join the local police force so that I could do what I believed I was supposed to as a married man. When I told my parents about my grand plan, they wanted no part of it.

    So, my dad took me to a Navy recruiter to see about enlisting in the Navy, as he had done when he left home at the age of seventeen. This Navy recruiter, however, must have met his quota for the next decade! Despite an ASVAB score that would guarantee my acceptance, and my eagerness to enlist and move on with my life (and Debbie's), the man directed me back to UT and to the ROTC program there.

    Fine! I'll finish school.
    At least I now have a plan.

Worth Dying For
L. Todd Kelly

That summer I attended the Naval Science Institute (NSI) in Newport, Rhode Island, where I met my first Marine Corps Gunnery Sergeant. This experience, for those who have not had the pleasure, is not something I can describe in words. The best I can do is: Intense. The hair was cut to a "high and tight." That was only the first change.

I survived NSI and returned to the University of Texas. During my senior year of college, I went through Lutheran Catechism classes and joined the Lutheran church. I did that (like so many other things in my life) for a girl (Debbie) – rather than for Jesus. I was quickly offended by the "closed communion," as that seemed the antithesis of what I thought Jesus preached. I attended for a time but eventually left.

My remaining educational experience at UT was filled with a continuation of my walk-in-sin with as many women as I could coerce into my bedroom. My faithfulness to Debbie was less than complete. I graduated with a degree in journalism in 1987, and as soon as I completed Officer Candidate's School, I earned a commission as a Marine Corps Officer.

Now, I think, *I am a man.*

I ALSO EARNED THE RIGHT TO WEAR AN EMBLEM THAT MANY GREAT MEN BEFORE ME BELIEVED, AS I NOW DID, WAS WORTH DYING FOR.

Worth Dying For
L. Todd Kelly

FATHER'S LOVE. A Father's Love needs to be one of example—both in how to treat a romantic partner, but also in how to be treated by one.

FATHER'S LIFE. A Father's Life should exemplify a reverence for God, not for the affection of any human, including women.

FATHER'S FEAR. A Father's Fear that their children become too immersed in the desire for human affection and thereby ignore the commands of the Father who has commanded otherwise.

FATHER'S FIGHT. A Father's Fight is to live his life in a manner that points his children toward God, and not to demonstrate giving in to his own fleshly desires.

FATHER'S WISDOM. A Father's Wisdom should lead his children to love God, rather than the affection of the opposite sex.

THE ILLUSION OF PURPOSE AND PERFECTION
7

The Brave

A well-conditioned body, chiseled by hard work
A sense of duty, that none of us would shirk.
The neatly trimmed appearance and the short, well-cut hair,
Were proof that we were part of a history we'd share.

Pride, they say, comes before a good man's fall
But that couldn't happen – not to one if not to all.
This Corps has stood so proudly, and we've instilled so much fear
And now I wear the emblem too, as I stand right here.

We were young and strong, and proud, and we knew it too.
But most of all we knew the power of our uniforms of blue.
We simply donned a uniform made legend by the past,
And we'd enjoy its spoils as long as that would last.

We even fooled ourselves with the oaths that we all took
We thought our integrity and courage could not be shook.
In boldness now we stepped into a life – intent to serve,
Our training, and our boldness – yeah, we had some nerve.

And dragging others in so that we would not be alone,
To make them pay a price for which we would not atone.
But we had no guilt and knew no shame for dragging them along,
They each came willingly with us, as we sang our little song.

•••••••••••

Worth Dying For
L. Todd Kelly

**JULY 10, 1987,
QUANTICO, VIRGINIA.**

I HAD JUST COMPLETED Officer Candidate's School or OCS. Trained by another Marine Gunnery Sergeant ("Gunny") and a Staff Sergeant, my body was ripped, but my mind was even harder. I was a proud American that day!

**I KNEW THAT I SERVED A COUNTRY...
WORTH DYING FOR.**

My parents, Jim and Linda, and my younger brother, Reagan, flew in from Texas to be with me as I took my oath of office. I recall the pride as my mother pinned my "butter bars" on the collar of my "Charlies." The love and adoration in the eyes of my mother made all the pull-ups, push-ups, mountain climbers, and other forms of legal torture worth it. Her little boy had just become a Marine Lieutenant.

Lieutenant of Marines. I sought that title for several years after my father convinced me not to join the police force. Now it had arrived. I would attend six months of The Basic School at Quantico, then out into the fleet to do – whatever the needs of the Marine Corps demanded.

My dad had never been so proud. But I wouldn't fully realize the extent of that pride for a few years. Still, that day I felt the approval of this man whose approval has always meant so much to me.

Worth Dying For
L. Todd Kelly

As I stood in patriotic glory and the loving adoration of my family, I took an oath–a solemn promise to my country. An oath which I would take with each subsequent advancement in rank:

I do solemnly swear that I will support and defend the Constitution of the United States against all enemies, foreign and domestic; that I will bear true faith and allegiance to the same; that I take this obligation freely, without any mental reservation or purpose of evasion; and that I will well and faithfully discharge the duties of the office on which I am about to enter. So help me God.

At the Officers Basic Course in Quantico (The Basic School), I achieved enough success in my training to give me some say in my career choice.

**I HAD FRIENDS I BELIEVED WERE ...
WORTH DYING FOR.**

Of course, they felt the same way about me, right?

I also met Marysue, the daughter of a retired Navy Captain. She was a pretty, young, vibrant, happy brunette. The first night I met her, I was out with several friends from The Basic School at a bar in Alexandria, Virginia. Her first words to me are not hard to recall:

"Are you a Marine?"

"This is going to be a good night!" I thought to myself, expecting that with a question like that she would be easy to bed.

Worth Dying For
L. Todd Kelly

Turns out Marysue was just making sure she knew the actual branch of service that my high and tight haircut was attributable to.

She was smart, and she was attractive. But I had other plans for my life, so I really didn't have more than a night to offer her. She asked to see my military ID to prove that I was a Marine and not just posing. I showed it. We had a nice chat, then—despite my best efforts—that was the end of it…

A week later, Marysue called the duty officer for "Golf" Company—my company at TBS. She had memorized my social security number from my ID card and used her father's military connections to track me down! With an unforgettable name like "Marysue," I knew that the duty officer wasn't kidding when he gave me the message that she called.

After several all-night phone conversations on a pay phone in the squad bay later (followed by exhaustive all-day training sessions), I started really falling for this girl. She seemed to have dreams and aspirations that were similar to my own; and as a bonus, she laughed at my terrible jokes. The sexual banter between us was intoxicating.

As the time for selection of Military Occupational Specialties (aka job assignments) was upon me, I had earned the right to select 9th among my classmates. I was told that I could essentially have any job I want in the Corps. I wanted to fly Cobra helicopters (my father had worked for Bell Helicopter, and many of my childhood heroes flew "choppers"), but my poor vision would surely have me washed out of flight school and

Worth Dying For
L. Todd Kelly

the Corps would then just choose for me – according to its needs. Also, I had learned, much to my dismay, that the Cobra was not a Marine Corps asset, and I was not interested in flying for the Army.

While I could still have some influence over this life decision, I decided to select the MOS of 1302: Combat Engineer Officer. After all, I liked going to the field with the grunts, but what I really liked was blowing things up. I was like a kid with a new toy, only these toys were C4 explosives!

The idea of being a lawyer was not within my sights anymore at this point.

Marysue and I dated for the remainder of my time in Quantico. I frequently drove to Alexandria, Virginia, where her parents graciously allowed me to stay in their downstairs bedroom. Her father would sit just outside that room watching sports most nights, in a failed attempt to keep my hands off his daughter. We were in our early 20s and physically attracted to each other: no place was safe.

Our relationship grew into much more than the one night I had originally envisioned. Not only was I attracted to her physically, but we could talk about virtually anything. It became very comfortable.

My friends at The Basic School didn't understand that this was getting serious and proved that by hitting on her when we would all go out together. My roommate, Frank, bought her a rose one night to gain her attention. So, naturally, in a barbaric display of testosterone and to ensure that Marysue never

Worth Dying For
L. Todd Kelly

received the intended come-on, I ate that rose right off the stem. Made my point, but for reference: roses taste horrible!

My officer training continued at Combat Engineer Officer's School at Courthouse Bay, in Camp LeJeune, North Carolina. Serving with Marines I would die for is the most American thing I could imagine doing at this point in my life. Except on the weekends, that is. Those days were reserved for my conjugal visits with Marysue.

I got my orders before graduation from Combat Engineer School.

I was assigned to go to Hawaii to be the engineer officer for BSSG-1.

Then, it hit me: if I am serious about Marysue, I had better hurry up and marry her. So, in six short months after meeting her, Marysue and I tied the knot in a military wedding at Fort Belvoir Virginia. The wedding was small, but our families and close friends were there. (It was that or leave her, as I would get orders to Hawaii, and they don't put girlfriends on your military orders).

EVERYTHING SEEMED PERFECT.
A WIFE AND A CAREER THAT WERE BOTH...
WORTH DYING FOR.

Worth Dying For
L. Todd Kelly

FATHER'S LOVE. A Father's Love requires putting others ahead of himself.

FATHER'S LIFE. A Father's Life should be devoted to his children, but also to his wife.

FATHER'S FEAR. A Father's Fear requires that he understand that the danger in which he puts himself is also a danger that his family endures.

FATHER'S FIGHT. A Father's Fight is to ensure that he puts his family ahead of his own desires.

FATHER'S WISDOM. A Father's Wisdom requires that he keep pride in check and that he boast about only one thing—Jesus.

ABOUT DAMNED TIME

8

SEMPER FI

The sweat-stained faces of
determined men
Surround them like a lion's
den.
The objective lies in plain
view now.
The enemy does not know
how.

Training days in Quantico
Were long and cold—with
ice and snow.
We knew we wouldn't spend
our life
Without some wear, some
toil, some strife.

We understood that the price
some paid
For freedom was one we'd
freely trade.
Sacrifice, Esprit de Corps
Were what we wanted, and
what's more…

We flew our colors high and
proud.
We teased, we taunted, we
yelled out loud.
The life we chose was not of
ease.
But rather one to pay for
peace.

Raised in this land where
freedom rings,
We understood we'd feel the
stings.

We knew when we cried
"Semper Fi,"
That some of us were meant
to die.

But not this Jarhead, not
today.
I never thought that price I'd
pay.
But our brothers, sisters, I
knew they might.
And for their lives agree to
fight.

So sleep in peace beloved
land.
We are prepared to fight in
sand.
Lay down your head and
know you'll wake.
The other lives are what we'll
take.

My brother warriors, train
today
So that we forge and make a
way.
That freedom for our fellow
man
Is bought because we care,
we can.

All enemies from there or
here,
Let me make this very clear:
For freedom we know some
must die.
U.S. Marines. Semper Fi.

• • • • • • • • • • •

Worth Dying For
L. Todd Kelly

I SPENT THE NEXT three years stationed at Marine Corps Air Station, Kaneohe (as it was known at the time), "K-Bay" for short.

I was assigned to Brigade Service Support Group-1 in 1988. The executive officer of BSSG-1 was LtCol Joseph Composto, a Judge Advocate serving in a fleet leadership role at the time. I was fortunate, as I will later learn, to have met him and to have had the opportunity to brief him on the engineering capabilities of our unit during a field training operation at the Pohakaloa Training Area on the Big Island of Hawaii. This man would eventually rise to the rank of General, and become the Judge Advocate General (JAG) of the Marine Corps.

As I checked in to the Landing Support Company and was assigned to the Engineer detachment that I would command, I was overwhelmed by the responsibility. At 23 years of age, I was entrusted to lead 110 Marines and take responsibility for over $12 Million worth of military equipment. No pressure—but I did not let it show…

Gunnery Sergeant (Gunny) Robert Smith was my senior enlisted man and knew as soon as he laid eyes on me that he had to train another "Damned Butter Bar." Gunny Smith and I had conversations about the direction we wanted the detachment to be led. He knew full well that while I was the officer in charge, I could not do my job without him. I knew it, too.

As responsibility increased at work, things at home became stressful. Marysue and I had been involved in infertility treatment for some time. We both

Worth Dying For
L. Todd Kelly

wanted to be parents, but we had been unsuccessful. Every late period brought hope, which was only shattered days later when her cycle would start. We saw doctors, we tried "red light, green light" days (not the most romantic means of intimacy), and we did virtually everything we read about. Still, no baby.

At work, I listened to the Gunny. I watched him. I learned from him. In doing so, my Marines become just that – my Marines. It happened subtly, over time. We were running in formation a year or so after I took the detachment, and I decided during the run that we would run up Kansas Tower (the historic hill where Navy radiomen in the radio tower first saw the Japanese suicide bombers as they made their way toward Pearl Harbor to bring the United States into WWII), which we affectionately called "KT."

But Gunny Smith contradicted me, "No, Sir. We are going to run to the rifle range today."

This was a point of no return: the Gunny had just told me, his Lieutenant, in front of our Marines, that he would not follow me. The fork in the road was both literal and symbolic. If we turned left (KT), they were following me. If we turned right (Rifle Range), they were not.

I directed my next order to the guide (a Marine who carries the banner that the entire formation will follow):

"Marine, you follow me or you're losing a stripe today! That is an order, do you understand?"

Worth Dying For
L. Todd Kelly

When Gunny turned right at the fork as he said he would, I turned left.

The guide stutter-stepped but followed me and his lawful order—towards KT. The formation, in turn, followed the guide. We ran KT that day.

The Gunny turned around and caught back up to me at the head of the formation. He was grinning as big as I had ever seen him grin.

"It's about damned time, sir!

My training, in his eyes, was complete.

At home, another task had become complete. We had just learned that Marysue was pregnant after our last round of invitro. I was going to be a Daddy, after all!

A couple of weeks later, I learned that there was more: I would be a Daddy—of twins. But our little world was not the whole picture…

On the other side of the globe, Saddam Hussein had started a war in Iraq (the country bordering the one in which I had spent those four formative years.) This was the call that I trained for, and I expected to lead my Marines into harm's way. This would need my full attention. I was ready and up for the call. We knew the risk. We knew that my unborn children may never know their father. But we also knew that Hussein was using chemical weapons—even on his own people.

This was the moment we had trained for, and we would continue to prepare. I had never been gassed with so much CS gas as I was during that life-saving

Worth Dying For
L. Todd Kelly

preparation. CS gas is akin to tear gas. It is used to train our military combatants to use their nuclear, biological, and chemical defense gear properly. It is also used to provide some sense of confidence in the masks that we wear to protect ourselves.

So, to ensure we were ready to survive the deadly chemicals at Hussein's disposal, we prepared by exposing ourselves to this painful substance.

But the real tears filled my eyes when my twins, Joshua Ryan, and Meghan Brough, were born early at the Kapiolani Medical Center in Honolulu in June of 1990, at only 27 weeks gestation. Physicians urged abortion because of the likelihood of significant medical issues and likely early death in children born prematurely. Marysue and I had to make a difficult choice that day about the lives of our unborn children. I hated this choice.

These little people, whom I had never actually met, were already worth more than my own life to me. I could not end theirs. After all, my mother likely received that same advice at the tender age of 16 years, and I am still here—with everything I have put her through. I wondered, *perhaps there are days she doubts that decision.*

My ignorance of the significance of that early birth saved me from the full force of fear about what my children faced due to their prematurity. By God's grace, I was completely ignorant of the risks related to their prognoses and medical challenges at the time of having *one-pounders.*

Worth Dying For
L. Todd Kelly

Ironic that I would later become a birth injury trial lawyer, well-versed in those challenges. I spent my evenings, every one of them, scrubbed down and looking at these little children that I loved more than I had ever known possible. My own children, who are worth everything to me. I prayed for them. I was willing to do anything for them to survive. If it were God's will, I offered in prayer to take their place. They were worth trading my life for more than anything I had ever known.

The focus on the survival of these wonders from God was stressful for Marysue and me. We didn't really see it at first, as we were both so tired from just getting to the hospital and praying for their very survival, but we were not focused on each other. I assumed she would just be there, and she knew I would be.

Although I didn't know the reason at first, I was ordered to the flight line at Pearl Harbor to assist in the deployment of all Marines out of Kaneohe into the theater of operations in Iraq for what would be Operation Desert Storm and Desert Shield. As a detachment commander for the company responsible for logistics, that role was not unusual. I eventually loaded my Marines on a plane destined for the combat zone with an honest promise that I was three days behind them.

"See you in country, Gunny,"

"See you in country, Gunny," were the last words I spoke to the man who had devoted so much time to train me as a young lieutenant, not knowing if we would be reconnected "in country," or ever.

Worth Dying For
L. Todd Kelly

I returned to the makeshift flightline office in my shipping container and watched my Marines ascend into the blue Hawaiian sky. I could still see the plane in the air when my relief, a lieutenant, ironically also named Smith, walked in. "The colonel wants to see you, Kelly."

My heart sank. I knew what it meant: I wouldn't keep my promise to the Gunny.

"I can still see 'em," I urged Lieutenant Smith about my Marines—as if he could have somehow controlled the colonel's decision.

I pleaded with the colonel about my Marines and how I needed to be with them, but he was unrelenting in his decision to leave me behind.

"You have two babies in the NICU, Lieutenant," he explained.

"They need you, and I don't need a distracted officer in the field."

"I won't ask to come home, sir!"

"And I'm not <u>asking</u> you to stay, Lieutenant."

Again, God's grace was on me – though I could not see it. Instead, I viewed it, at that moment, as anything but. I served during Desert Shield and Desert Storm – but not in it. I admittedly was bitter about that decision I didn't have a say in.

After almost eight long and trying months, my Marines returned from the desert in Iraq to Hawaii and

Worth Dying For
L. Todd Kelly

let me know that they always knew my heart – and that I wanted to be with them. I was dedicated to the Corps.

I WAS A *LIFER* IN THIS FRATERNITY
WORTH DYING FOR
—OR SO I STILL THOUGHT.

Worth Dying For
L. Todd Kelly

FATHER'S LOVE. A Father's Love is a powerful and instinctive love that embodies sacrifice and commitment above almost every other.

FATHER'S LIFE. A Father's Life must be a sacrifice to his children – above all else.

FATHER'S FEAR. A Father's Fear is that his children are not well protected and provided for.

FATHER'S FIGHT. A Father's Fight ensures that he puts his own desires aside for his children – regardless of how noble those desires may be.

FATHER'S WISDOM. A Father's Wisdom should guide his decisions so that he leaves an example for his children to follow.

BE CAREFUL WHAT YOUR PRAY FOR

9

Dreams

You dream of something all your life,
Then at the end of strife,
An chance is given to reach your goal
What is the cost, what is the toll?

You may not know the price you'll pay,
So for now, just enjoy your day.

Do not think of all you've lost
Or even of the future cost.

Your mission now almost complete,
So, on another field, compete.
Are you the one you think you are?
Get ready, goals are often far.

•••••••••••

I WAS reassigned to Cherry Point, North Carolina, as the Engineer Officer for Marine Wing Support Squadron—271. While serving in this capacity, I applied to the Marine Corps Funded Law Education Program (for a third time.) When I first accepted my commission, I had no idea that becoming an attorney through the Marine Corps was an option. It now appeared that I had an opportunity to fulfill my childhood dream of being a lawyer—perhaps I could be the next *Perry Mason* or *Matlock*.

It was hard to compete with combat veterans for the honor of being selected to law school in this competitive program. I was, after all, not in the war zone during our most recent victory. This time, however, Colonel Keith Sefton, the Staff Judge Advocate at Cherry Point, North Carolina, wrote a tremendous recommendation letter after I interviewed him. I had a real shot!

Worth Dying For
L. Todd Kelly

Weeks of anxious anticipation passed, waiting for the board's decision. There was a delay for some unknown reason.

"Captain Kelly," came the voice of a Marine Major that I had been waiting for, "I have good news – and bad."

My heart sank into the pit of my stomach, "Yes, sir?"

"You were accepted." My spirit lifted.

"And the bad?" I asked – that part must have been a joke!

"We had to cancel the funded program this year because of funding cutbacks, but you can still go—if you pay for it —on the Excess Leave Program."

"Ooh Rah!"

Worth Dying For
L. Todd Kelly

FATHER'S LOVE. A Father's Love must not be lost in his struggle to set an example.

FATHER'S LIFE. A Father's Life combines his personal progress and leading his family.

Father's Fear. A Father's Fear is that he may be lost in the daily routines of life.

FATHER'S FIGHT. A Father's Fight is to provide for his family and to remember that he is also a son.

FATHER'S WISDOM. A Father's Wisdom requires knowing when he has taken on too much.

BREAKUPS, BREAKDOWNS AND BREAKTHROUGHS

—— 10 ——

LEGAL FICTION

The laws are written on these pages,
Handed down throughout the ages.
Brilliant minds stood in these halls,
Their photographs adorn the walls.

This musty curtilage and winding stairs
Could tell the history it shares
With lawyers from the early days,
Who've changed our courts, our laws, our ways.

To stand among these hallowed walks
And listen to the well-honed talks,
I'm not so sure that I belong,
But I won't tell them they were wrong.

I've listened as professors teach,
I feel that someday I may reach
The confidence to stand and talk,
To truly walk this lawyer's walk.

Ego's here so easily fed,
But ego's better if it just lies dead.

Resumes built here, line by line,
What will I put down next on mine?

This school is building me up so much,
Yet, truly, it's keeping me out of touch
Reality isn't in our schooling,
It's hard to imagine the long re-tooling,

With time these legal facts and codes
May fade as ego then erodes.
But will the damage to my soul,
Leave more than just a gaping hole?

Graduating, honors, airborne caps,
We dream success and all its traps,
How foolish are those things of youth,
But time always reveals its truth.

The sins committed without regard,
Excuses that the law is hard.
Escape lasts for but a passing time,
It isn't worth the fleeting crime.

August 1992,
Carlisle, Pennsylvania.

I arrived at the Dickinson School of Law in Carlisle, Pennsylvania. Founded in 1834, Dickinson is the oldest law school in Pennsylvania and one of the oldest in the nation. It was rich in tradition.

I walked to class past the rich mahogany stairwell and took in the musty smell of the curtilage. The photos of barristers long since passed gave an air of distinction to the entryway and halls. This school gave dignity to the law in much the traditional way I expected. I felt a twinge of self-doubt and insecurity as I looked up and down the old wooden staircase.

Am I in over my head?
Do I really have what it takes to learn the law?
Do I really belong here?

There was no turning back. I had been accepted by Dickinson – an honor in itself, but I was ordered here by the United States Marine Corps. This was my duty now.

Do your job.

This was my new duty station because I was still considered an active-duty Marine. I took to this new job of learning the law like a Marine was supposed to —with determined vigor and a desire to be the best at my new mission.

It was not lost on me when we sat in the large auditorium on the first day and were informed about the impressive credentials of this incoming class of law

Worth Dying For
L. Todd Kelly

students: the valedictorians, salutatorians, Rhodes scholars, and others who sat among us. All top students from major universities. We were an impressive assembly of over-achievers. The dean instructed us to look to our right, then to our left, to take in the level of achievement (and arrogance) sitting in that room. Then, with cold, mathematical certainty that he clearly enjoyed, he informed us:

HALF OF YOU WILL BE IN THE BOTTOM HALF OF YOUR CLASS.

The reality of that harsh truth may have taken the wind out of my sails, but only temporarily.

Marysue, Josh, and Meghan accompanied me to Carlisle. It was close enough to both of our parents so the kids' grandparents could enjoy quality time with Josh and Meghan as I spent my time buried in my studies. Marysue was used to moving around as a military dependent her entire life, so she took this move in stride.

The concept of civil law was foreign to me as a Marine Officer. This became very clear in my first semester when Professor Michael Mogill, my Torts professor, asked me if I understood the holding in the "Spring Gun Case."

For those who have not studied the law, a *tort* is not a pastry. It is, quite simply, a civil wrong, normally based on negligence or reckless behavior. The holding

Worth Dying For
L. Todd Kelly

of a case, for those unfamiliar with the concept, is the particular principle the case stands for.

The *spring gun* case involved a man collecting antique cologne bottles in an unoccupied shed on his land. Kids would break in when the building was vacant and steal the bottles and vandalize the shed. To stop these young thieves, the landowner set up and loaded a shotgun to go off when the unsuspecting thieves broke into the shed. It worked, costing one of the young thieves half his leg.

"Yes, I know the holding."

"Please tell us the holding, Mr. Kelly."

The Marine in me responded, "Aim two feet higher!"

Disappointed but perhaps slightly amused, Professor Mogill explained that human life is always more important than property. Is it?

THESE THIEVES HAD COMMITTED A CRIME THAT I BELIEVED WAS WORTH DYING FOR.

This was the first step in a transformation that I never saw coming.

As it turns out, he was not wrong. At the time, however, I only knew I wanted to prosecute criminals. Although well aware that other types of lawyers existed, I could see no other value for lawyers other than to remove criminals from our society. It would be years before I understood civil trial lawyers, and still a

Worth Dying For
L. Todd Kelly

couple of years before I recognized that criminal defense lawyers differ from the crimes they defend others of. I had a lot to learn.

Law school was stressful. As the dean pointed out, half of us would be in the bottom half of the class, and some would fail. These were people from the very top of their academic worlds.

Am I that failure?
Am I perhaps a fraud, after all?

Perhaps I was just fooling myself into thinking I had what it took to be there with those people. My confidence was shaken to its core.

Worth Dying For
L. Todd Kelly

FATHER'S LOVE. A Father's Love must not be lost in his personal struggles.

FATHER'S LIFE. A Father's Life requires a focus on his family that can seem in conflict with the world's demands.

FATHER'S FEAR. A Father's Fear is that he may lose his way of pursuing his chosen professional obligations.

FATHER'S FIGHT. A Father's Fight is to walk the line between providing for his family as well as he can while teaching the virtues that are Godly.

FATHER'S WISDOM. A Father's Wisdom requires that he devote appropriate amounts of time to each role he must play.

Worth Dying For
L. Todd Kelly

FAILURE TO EVOLVE

11

Pathways

Changing wasn't my intent,
Just to graduate, my bent.
So why, then, did I fall to sin,
And let my own downfall begin?

I'd come so far and changed so much,
Am I really weakened by one touch?
But that is all it seems to take,
For my very soul to crack and shake.

The sinful nights that we both share
Have left my inner self so bare
I failed my covenant to keep,
A better man could never sleep.

The lies I told myself were wrong,
I'd hear my justice in some song.
I convinced myself, "I'm just a man."
Besides, I'm doing all I can.

But Satan's lies that I adorned
Could not appease the way they scorned.
The scorn I earned with each new sin,
The losses that I thought a "win."

My own father had to sit me down,
As I had made my sin renown.
And though that meeting felt so strange,
I heard his words and tried to change.

A path back to the life I knew,
And maybe some forgiveness, too.
But arrogance had made me blind,
I left that path so far behind.

As I held on to yet another,
I joined my uniformed sister, brother.
I would bury me in service now,
Ignoring my holy, solemn vow.

••••••••••

Worth Dying For
L. Todd Kelly

I STARTED to change during that first year. I spent long hours with my study group. The late nights, occasional drinks, and long study hours had the four of us leaning on each other quite a bit. I became close with all three, but when one of the women seemed interested in me for more than a legal analysis, my old insecurities revealed themselves again. She seemed attracted to me.

I knew it was wrong —I was married. Still, I couldn't help feeling the attraction of someone else's desire. Things at home had not been the same with the stress of the twins' premature birth, living through a war, then law school acceptance, and now the many hours devoted to studying law. Marysue was busy with the kids, and I was busy with school. There was no romance there.

I had an affair with this girl that was quickly discovered by the others in the group. Despite the guilt that accompanied the affair, I did not turn from it because it fueled my ego in a way that I felt I somehow needed. As guilty as I felt about this affair, I didn't stop.

It was an escape from the stress of law school and the fear of failure that had shrouded my once-confident demeanor. It shrouded me in a false confidence in my attractiveness. It became an obsession and my primary focus. I convinced myself that I needed this. I even convinced myself that I deserved this moment, these times of escape with her. I had turned my back to God, and I didn't even want Him to see me.

Marysue discovered the affair. Not that it was a harrowing discovery, as law students tend to gossip worse than old ladies at a hair salon. We contemplated

Worth Dying For
L. Todd Kelly

divorce. She even packed her bags and took Josh and Meghan back to her parent's home in Virginia. I held my twins as she packed her bags and wondered, "What have I done?" I had never cried harder. But my tears didn't stop her. I deserved this.

I DIDN'T BELIEVE OUR MARRIAGE COULD BE FIXED, SO I DIDN'T TRY TO STOP HER.

Her words formed her only question: "How could you?"

I could not answer that question. I honestly didn't know, myself. I was also keenly aware that one phone call to my command about what I had done would end my Marine Corps career and my chance at being a lawyer.

Instead, Marysue called my parents. I was shocked when Dad showed up in Carlisle unannounced to take me to breakfast. I was almost as shocked when he ordered coffee at our local diner. Although he would make my mother's coffee every morning for years, he never drank it. He said he liked the smell but not the taste. Still, there was a black cup of coffee in front of him, and he was drinking it. It was the first and the last cup of coffee I have ever seen him drink.

The look on my father's face said it all. He was disappointed. That much was clear. But he was trying to help. He somehow understood that I had already beat myself up, so he didn't come for that. He just

Worth Dying For
L. Todd Kelly

showed me love and acceptance. He showed me a father's love –when I did not deserve it.

In the end, Marysue and I decided that our children needed a stable home and a lot of family involvement, so we tried to patch things up. It worked – for a time. It was difficult at first. She understandably didn't want to touch the man who betrayed her. We would have to work to rebuild this marriage. Trust was gone. That aspect of our relationship would never wholly return.

At the end of my first year of law school, I returned to Cherry Point, North Carolina, to work under Colonel Sefton's direction. I was extremely honored and excited to work under the man who had opened the door to allow me to finally fulfill my dream of being a lawyer.

Colonel Sefton allowed me to work with the prosecutors and even permitted me to personally prosecute a few of those "scum bags" who dared to violate the Uniform Code of Military Justice while wearing the uniform I valued so highly. Given my own guilt of not only the crime of adultery (adultery is a crime, actually, under the Uniform Code of Military Justice) but also my clear violation of one of the Ten Commandments, it is ironic that I could still be so judgmental of the offenses of others.

I returned to Dickinson for my second year of law school. Again, I worked hard and was selected to compete on trial and appellate moot court teams and the Jessup International Law Moot Court Team. I was even elected to serve on the student bar association as a class representative! I was gaining confidence in my

Worth Dying For
L. Todd Kelly

knowledge of the law almost daily, making my way to being the best prosecutor I could be. However, my confidence in my own human morality was waning. After all, how could I profess to love my family yet betray them? What kind of a man does that? I buried those feelings of self-loathing. They were not productive, and I was building an impressive law student resume.

In the summer before my third (and final) year of law school, I served my "summer fun" duty at Quantico, Virginia, which exposed me to some pretty mundane issues like people suing for money against the military exchange, vehicle crashes, and several other civil law issues that I simply didn't care about. I didn't understand the devastation of a civil wrong – yet.

In my third year of law school, I was selected for an internship with the Cumberland County District Attorney's office. I was assigned to work with Jonathan Birbeck, a Senior Assistant District Attorney whom I had watched in trial during one of our class trips to the courthouse – someone whose courtroom skill I admired greatly. Jon even let me prosecute some of the misdemeanor cases entirely on my own – let me put some pretty evil prostitutes and marijuana users in jail.

The first prostitute that I came up against at a preliminary hearing had been picked up in a sting operation by an undercover cop. He posed as a "John" and arrested her when she named her price.

Expecting Julia Roberts from _Pretty Woman_ to walk into the courtroom that day, I prepared myself to hold back my prurient interests in this woman. That

Worth Dying For
L. Todd Kelly

was not necessary. I was surprised to see the woman's appearance as she walked in. Years of methamphetamine and cocaine use, combined with living on the streets, had taken their toll on this poor soul that had long since lost any pleasant physical attributes. Instead, I wondered, "How could anyone find that attractive enough to pay for it?"

Though barely coherent enough to speak, she was left to defend herself. After she was confined to await bail or trial, the DA's office congratulated me for winning my first hearing. I felt like a real lawyer!

TODAY, WITH THE BENEFIT OF HINDSIGHT, I AM ASHAMED TO HAVE TAKEN PART IN THE HUMAN TRAGEDY THAT THESE CHILDREN OF GOD ENDURED.

I am even more ashamed that I thought I had the right to judge this unfortunate woman. That right was never mine.

Having *patched up* our marriage, I soon learned that Marysue was expecting our third child and second son, Matthew Stewart, would be born during my third year of law school. This time, there was no need for fertility drugs or treatments—it just happened. Our relationship, while still on the mend, was better as well.

We made friends with other couples at the law school; one couple even had kids the age of Josh and Meghan. This helped to keep our focus on the family and our relationship. It also helped to re-kindle our

Worth Dying For
L. Todd Kelly

romantic feelings for each other, leading to Matthew's conception.

This was a good time for it, as the third year is much less stressful than the first two. The running joke used to describe the three years of law school is that they "*Scare* you to death, then work you to death, then bore you to death." Having a newborn made that third year anything but boring. Unlike his siblings, Matthew didn't have to spend months in a NICU; he could take a bottle the first day he came home. He was a healthy, happy baby, bringing far more joy than stress. Watching cartoons with him in my lap while having a cup of coffee seemed to replace the need to be wanted by other women.

I graduated from Dickinson as a member of the Woolsack Honor Society, top 10% of the class. Then on to take the bar exam in Virginia. The ultimate stressful exam – two full days of testing (some places have three). I traveled to Roanoke with my friend, Tracy Steele, to take the exam. Pass, and I would be a lawyer. Fail, and I would not. I wouldn't know for months.

Before I got my bar exam results, I was sent to Newport, Rhode Island, to attend Naval Justice School. For three months, I learned the ropes of being a new military judge advocate and, kindly, had a couple of months to get back in shape before we were to report back to the fleet. I was enjoying the courses, and the reshaping of my law school physique, until…

I met a pretty young Naval Officer who was my classmate. She was shy but funny, and she was brilliant. I was immediately attracted but kept my distance at

Worth Dying For
L. Todd Kelly

first. After all, things were finally better at home! We became friends during the three-month school, and I fell for her —hard. Again, I chose to ignore God as He told me to stay away. This one, I thought, I was truly in love with. I added yet another to a growing line of sins that He paid for because of my selfish desires and lack of foresight to realize the damage I was doing both to my marriage and to my soul. I ignored all of that and let myself fall for this woman—and I let her fall for me, knowing that we each had orders to different parts of the world and that this could not continue.

Then, without knowing if I had passed the bar exam, I was sent to my first duty station since law school to begin my work as a judge advocate.

Hawaii, again! I was told, "no" when I asked if I could return. But I was not complaining!

THIS WAS A DUTY STATION WORTHY OF DYING FOR.

Worth Dying For
L. Todd Kelly

FATHER'S LOVE. A Father's Love must not be traded for temporary highs – of any kind.

FATHER'S LIFE. A Father's Life is dedicated to his family, and a betrayal of that dedication is a betrayal of the entire family.

FATHER'S FEAR. A Father's Fear is that he be lost to sin.

FATHER'S FIGHT. A Father's Fight is to walk away from Satan's allure, no matter how attractive it may be in the moment.

FATHER'S WISDOM: A Father's Wisdom requires that he know that God has a greater plan for him and that he is required to follow it or lose his very soul.

THE #1 RULE OF DEATH PENALTY SCHOOL

— 12 —

THE FEWER, THE PROUDER

The "Dream Team" that we thought we were,
The animosity we'd stir,
Defending Marines, most of the time
Less wrong than those who charged the crime.

Overcharging to them, a game
And so we fought with little shame.
Marines who'd made some small mistake,
Whose lives were now what stood at stake.

The arrogance of those who charged
The egos that it seemed enlarged,
Would they have found themselves so haughty,
If the world new about their naughty?

What of the perverse U.S. Attorney?
Who seemed on an unending journey
To bed as many wives of others,
Wives, or sisters, of even mothers?
He sits in his unshaken spot,
While destruction to others was his plot.
He'd laugh as though it was some game,
Yet his indecency not tame.

Right and wrong—such a simple thought,
But the world would change from what it taught.
Those who held the office—right.
The rest of us to fight that might.

To be correct is not enough,
To fight for right you must be tough.
For even those whose righteous cause,
Inspires hope, I caution, pause…

The fight will not always be won
By those who righteousness do don,
But sometimes when you refuse to quit,
Right may just pull out of.

There is good and there is dark,
But if you care to be a spark,
Recall that sparks are bright, then gone,
But sometimes, fire lingers on.

••••••••••••

Worth Dying For
L. Todd Kelly

SEPTEMBER 1995, MARINE CORPS BASE, KANEOHE, HAWAII

NOT SURE WHY THE name changed, but it was the same place I already knew so well.

I arrived at the Legal Service Center, this time as a Marine Captain, to receive my first assignment as an attorney. I immediately asked to be assigned as a prosecutor–'cause that's what any self-respecting Marine Corps Officer wants to be, right? "…let God sort 'em out!"

The staff-judge advocate of the base leaned back in her chair knowingly and asked, "I understand that you would like to be a prosecutor, is that correct, Captain Kelly?"

"Yes, ma'am."

"You're needed in defense."

Only later did I learn that after a lawyer cuts his (or her) teeth in the courtroom by defending Marines charged with crimes, will the government move him (or her) to the prosecution team, thus ensuring that the prosecutors are consistently more experienced in the courtroom than their adversaries charged with "defending these scum bags."

THE UNITED STATES CONSTITUTION AT ITS FINEST —BY OFFICERS WHO SWORE AN OATH THAT THE PARCHMENT ON WHICH IT WAS WRITTEN WAS WORTH DYING FOR.

Worth Dying For
L. Todd Kelly

The team consisted of four Marine Judge Advocates. Major Tom Hamilton, the Senior Defense Counsel, was a calm, collected officer who would later become a military judge. "Tommy Mo," as his contemporaries called him, was well-loved by most, but mainly by us—his defense team, Captain Kevin Mahne, a small, wiry guy who attended law school a year ahead of me on the Marine Corps Funded Legal Education Program, was the next ranking defense lawyer; Captain Arthur Wiggins, affectionately referred to as "AJ," a large man with a laugh that was even larger, and one of my best friends- or so I thought, was the most junior lawyer; and me.

The four of us made up for the disparity in experience with hard work and dedication to our clients. Despite our underdog position as the less experienced courtroom lawyers, our defense team won—a lot. In a satiric nod to the OJ Simpson defense lawyers, we called ourselves the *dream team*." Arrogance at its finest—and we knew it.

The *dream team* was hated by prosecutors and commanders all over the base. We were an island in this sea of Marines and therefore spent much of our time at work and during our off-duty hours together. Friday afternoons were spent in Major Hamilton's office, opening beers from the cooler he brought each Friday and discussing and reviewing our most complex cases. As we learned, we bonded, and we won.

AJ and I were particularly close. Each time he stood duty on the base, he came by the house and had dinner with my family. My kids adored him, and I

Worth Dying For
L. Todd Kelly

treasured the friendship. He was my brother. I had not had a closeness like that with another Marine. This was the legendary bond in our Corps but had been lacking in the Marine Corps…until AJ.

THIS WAS A BROTHER WORTH DYING FOR.

Worth Dying For
L. Todd Kelly

FATHER'S LOVE. A Father's Love sometimes requires a focus on providing for the family.

FATHER'S LIFE. A Father's Life should be devoted to his family and not to things of this world – even things that seem reasonable or just.

FATHER'S FEAR. A Father's Fear is that he will ultimately lose himself – but that is a part of being a good father.

FATHER'S FIGHT. A Father's Fight is putting his children ahead of his desires.

FATHER'S WISDOM. A Father's Wisdom is not boastful but quiet and restrained.

REALITY SUCKS

13

JUST US - SERVED

*We believed we'd leave
no man behind,
But daily that is all I'd
find.
The men that chose to
serve this land,
Discarded, with the slight
of hand.*

*Prosecutors lived to serve,
Commanders that simply
would not swerve
From the path that they
formed much to fast,
To make men pay for
things that passed.*

*These "men" – some still
in their teens,
Without the money or the
means
Were left with others
wearing clothes
Much like the ones that
covered those.*

*Justice was not the goal,
you see,
At least to many who
served with me.*

*The only ones who really
cared,
Were those accused –
and they were scared.*

*The tiny band of lawyers
fought,
With skills that we had
just been taught.
To save them from the
over-charge
The task, it seemed, was
way too large.*

*Life's distractions made it
worse,
Could I keep him from the
hearse?
Or would my focus on my
own life,
My deception, lies I told
my wife,*

*Steer me from the goal to
save,
Or was it normal to
behave
I knew I wasn't at my
best,
But blamed it all on this
job's stress.*

••••••••••••

Worth Dying For
L. Todd Kelly

I had the distinction of trying the first case in the Marine Corps regarding a new defense to the crime of *Carnal Knowledge*, or, in the civilian world, *statutory rape*. The new defense, called *mistake of fact*, was available, but the standard was high. The defendant had to prove that, at the time of the sexual conduct, he believed (reasonably) that the *victim* was at least eighteen years of age.

My nineteen-year-old client was coming out of the enlisted club at closing time after a night of drinking when two girls approached him. The girls were dressed in miniskirts and high heels and wearing heavy makeup. They appeared to have just come out of the club and showed interest in continuing their night.

The girls had decided to lose their virginity to a Marine leaving the club that night, and my client fit the bill. The girls introduced themselves to my client and his friend as eighteen and nineteen.

The *eighteen-year-old* asked to accompany my client to his barracks room to party, where she willingly gave him her virginity.

She was thirteen years old.

It was my sworn duty to defend this young man, and his mistake of fact appears reasonable and obvious, given his story.

I understood this defense and understood from my limited experience that if I failed to act quickly, the truth would be lost. I called both girls. I told them who I was and then told them I was recording the conversations. I asked each of them for their version of

Worth Dying For
L. Todd Kelly

events. They set forth the exact story my client had told me. I now knew he is innocent under the existing law.

The girls' fathers were both senior enlisted servicemen on their standing base. These dads were, understandably, irate at the sexual violations of their daughters but were somehow even angrier about my call to them in the performance of my sworn duty as the defense attorney.

These men expressed their mutual hatred for me as the jury handed down its verdict of *not guilty*. The girl lost her innocence, but this verdict saved a young Marine who would have otherwise been convicted of a crime he could not know he had committed.

The verdict for me?
I was hated even more.

Each member of the *dream team* was assigned the most significant case of our new careers. Four Marines were accused of killing a fifth—a capital offense. I was assigned to defend Alejandro Soto, the largest physical specimen of the accused. He had worked at the gym as his full-time duty! Alex, as he was called, was certainly not the mastermind behind this crime and didn't want much to do with it. But the government had its sights on him merely because he was physically large. Yep—that was the prosecution's apparent criteria for determining the mastermind behind this murder—who was the biggest guy?

HIS PARTICIPATION, THE PROSECUTORS DETERMINED, WAS WORTH DYING FOR.

Worth Dying For
L. Todd Kelly

I wisely requested more experienced counsel to be detailed, as I had not yet been a licensed attorney for a year.

Denied.
Unbelievable!

I wrote to the State Bar of Virginia (the only jurisdiction in which I was now licensed) to inquire whether the state that licensed me agreed that I was qualified to defend in a capital murder case with less than one year of experience.

Of course, I wasn't, and they admonished me so — in no uncertain terms. I subsequently reported the Commonwealth of Virginia's well-reasoned opinion to the Staff Judge Advocate.

Now she'll have to assign another, more seasoned, attorney to this murder case, right?
After all, doesn't the accused have the right to competent legal counsel?

Two weeks later, my answer arrived from the Virginia State Bar:

"The United States Government has determined that you meet the qualifications to defend Lance Corporal Alejandro Soto. Accordingly, the State Bar of Virginia finds that you are so qualified."—or words very close to those—the letter no longer exists.

After some pleading, I was sent to Newport, Rhode Island, to attend the Capital Defense Course. The only thing I truly remember from that course was that I had one objective: to keep Alex alive.

Worth Dying For
L. Todd Kelly

Well, I remember a beautiful Navy officer that I was still in love with, too. She happened to be attending the same course. We had dinner and enjoyed each other's company but refrained from intimacy, as we had seen the emotional damage done when we said goodbye the first time.

The critical lesson from Death Penalty School was to do whatever it took to keep your client alive. There wasn't much practical advice other than that.

I returned to Hawaii and defended Alex the best I could at my experience level (less than one year). To my relief, his life was spared. He was housed as a guest of the federal government for almost twenty years at Fort Leavenworth, Kansas—but he's alive.

Although I thought our team could never have been more hated than we already were, my wife was then called in to testify against a prosecutor who had been accused of sexually inappropriate conduct by the wife of the Provost Marshal (the head of the military police) on the base.

Marysue had been a dancer when she was younger, and Paul would frequently make strange, inappropriate comments about how *sexy* her feet were at social gatherings of the judge advocates on the base.

I could not understand how the legal community put its arms around Captain Paul Aroujo (a prosecutor) rather than the victim, who happened to be the wife of Captain L. Todd Kelly (a defense lawyer).

I understood why those untrained in the law hated me for the title I didn't request. Still, I couldn't

Worth Dying For
L. Todd Kelly

comprehend it from those who took the same oaths I took—and I certainly couldn't understand how they held my courtroom zeal against my wife, a victim of sexually inappropriate conduct.

Hypocrites, I thought.

When Marysue refused to lie to protect Captain Aroujo, the fallout from her involvement led to even more hatred among my peers in the legal service center.

Captain Aroujo was ultimately discharged for his misconduct. The repercussions of my wife's honesty would significantly impact the longevity of my career.

I WAS HATED EVEN MORE, BUT THE TRUTH WAS SOMETHING THAT I ARROGANTLY BELIEVED WAS WORTH DYING FOR.

Worth Dying For
L. Todd Kelly

Father's Love. A Father's Love belongs to his family and should not be directed outside the home.

Father's Life. A Father's Life should never involve other women and sinful distractions.

Father's Fear. A Father's Fear should be for the loss of his family and not for the loss of his own selfish ends.

FATHER'S FIGHT. A Father's Fight is to deny himself the momentary pleasures of life so that he can experience the fullness of fatherhood that he was first committed to.

FATHER'S WISDOM. A Father's Wisdom will keep him focused on his children and his wife and not let the distractions of this world turn him elsewhere.

WHEN THE TRUTH CAN NO LONGER BE DENIED

14

Brothers in Arms

The man I'd die for – my best friend,
The man I knew that in the end
Would stand for me – no matter what,
That's the brotherhood, we're taught.

His word his bond, and tightly sealed,
Until the truth, one day revealed.

He knows the truth, why won't he speak,
My head, he knows, is what they seek.

His lies, that he now holds so dear,
Will, in disgrace, cost my career.

Speak up, my friend, you loved me once,
Or was I just played to be your dunce?

You've taken sides, but not with truth.
I should have known, I am no youth.

You're not my brother, I see that now.
But it eludes me. I don't know how.

•••••••••••

A MARINE CORPORAL HAD been charged with stealing a government weapon, and his sergeant was charged with receiving that stolen property. AJ represented the Sergeant accused of receiving that stolen government property. I represented the Corporal accused of stealing the *government weapon*: ironically, a 9mm Beretta M9 pistol.

The Corporal had taken the pistol from the rifle range when another young Marine left it unattended at the 500-yard line. After he returned to the armory to check his weapons in, the Corporal stood in the back of

Worth Dying For
L. Todd Kelly

the line waiting for the young Marine to speak up so that he could admonish him about protecting his firearm, which could someday save his life. When no one spoke up, the Corporal, realizing that the idiot who lost the pistol must have been at the other armory, panicked and kept the pistol.

The Corporal, afraid, took the government-issued pistol to his Sergeant's off-base house because he didn't know what else to do. That's where the Criminal Investigation Division found the weapon and charged these two Marines with theft of a government weapon, though they were only guilty of stupidity. Neither of these Marines ever intended to commit a theft (known as *mens rea*).

> IT IS KNOWN THAT *THE ABSENCE OF INTENT* IS A SOLID LEGAL DEFENSE TO A THEFT CHARGE, AND I WAS PREPARED TO PUBLICLY EMBARRASS THE PROSECUTORS YET AGAIN.
> PERHAPS THAT PRIDE WAS MY UNDOING.

AJ stood with his innocent client as he entered a plea of guilty. Disappointed in that tact, I understood the risk and tried to keep my opinion to myself. I later asked my friend while working out at the gym if I could speak with his now-convicted client.

As he finished a set of inclined bench press, AJ responded, "I don't care. It's over for him, anyway."

Worth Dying For
L. Todd Kelly

A few weeks later, the former Sergeant, then a prisoner who had been reduced to the rank of private, was on base from the brig at Ford Island, and I was available to speak with him. AJ was not, but I had his permission. The former Sergeant swore out an affidavit which substantially set forth the story as my client had been telling me. There it was: reasonable doubt—in writing. I took the affidavit to the prosecutors to convince them to drop the charges against my client. I was expecting a dismissal of all charges, given the clear evidence of reasonable doubt that this affidavit creates.

However, Captain Wiggins (he ceased to be "AJ" to me at this point because of the actions he was about to take) returned to the Legal Services Center and told others that he never gave me the authority to speak with his client. I could not believe it. How could one of my best friends betray me like this—with a bald-faced lie?

Like buzzards swarming the decaying carcass of a dying beast, the prosecutors saw an opportunity to feed. A formal investigation was launched into my *ethical violation*. Within a week or so, the investigating officer arrived from Camp Pendleton, California, which brought a sinister joy to those in the legal center foaming at the mouth to end my career.

Though I had been ear-marked to take over as the Senior Defense Counsel ahead of the more senior Captain Mahne, the Regional Defense Counsel, LtCol John Canham, called me to let me know that there was simply too much happening around me to appoint me to that position, now. Captain Mahne would be assigned that role.

For reasons I could not quite understand, Wiggins was very friendly with the prosecutors who'd had it out for me all along! How had they become so close, I wondered. Of course, I knew the answer, but hated what it meant. He had chosen a side, and the truth did not matter.

THE TRUTH, AND THE FRIEND, BOTH OF WHOM I BELIEVED WERE WORTH DYING FOR, HAD BETRAYED ME.

Worth Dying For
L. Todd Kelly

FATHER'S LOVE. A Father's Love requires that he love his children, no matter how others treat him.

FATHER'S LIFE. A Father's Life should reflect goodness, even when he is struggling.

FATHER'S FEAR. A Father's Fear related to things outside the home should not affect how he treats his family at home.

FATHER'S FIGHT. A Father's Fight is outside the home and should not be brought into the house in front of his children.

FATHER'S WISDOM. A Father's Wisdom will help him survive his trials in this world, while remaining a dedicated servant to his family.

OUT OF THE FRYING PAN AND INTO THE FIRE

15

THE CUTS

Those we don't love cannot betray,
So the deepest cuts come in this way:
By those we've held in our hearts close
Those we've loved the very most.

When that one turns with "Judas' kiss"
And for the first time, you hear the hiss,
That one's bite does much more harm.
Is it because there's no alarm?

The cuts are deeper and the wounds heal slow,
In fact, sometimes, hatred will grow.
But as the hatred fills our thought
It's our own misery we've bought.

The trust we once gave out so free,
We now hold closer until we see
That those we would have trusted hence
We cannot trust – we build a fence.

This person did not cause my pain,
And though they try to reach, in vane,
Why would I block them out from me,
Is there something in them that I see?

Or is it simply fear of love,
Because I've drifted from above.
If God feared mine, as I deserve,
Then He would never let me serve.

If I'm to love like He has told,
Then I must trust, I must be bold.
So forward, as I must now travel,
I lay down my view – I drop my gavel.

Judgment wasn't mine to start,
I do not know what caused that heart,
To turn on me and cause my pain,
But I now choose to trust again.

••••••••••••

Worth Dying For
L. Todd Kelly

BEFORE THE ARRIVAL OF the investigating officer, I asked my *friend*, Captain Wiggins, to come and talk to me privately, man-to-man, in my office.

I had been moved to the wing of prosecutors at the legal service center. The furniture was nicer, and my office was quieter. I missed the defense side, but the Staff Judge Advocate moved me to avoid more issues. My office was about 100 yards from Wiggins' rather than next door as it had always been.

The light-stained faux wood furniture was the nicest I had in the Corps, and I was comfortable in this office, though not in my situation. The pace of my heart quickened as I heard Captain Wiggins' boots hitting the polished tile floors on his way to my office. I had never imagined that I would have to confront him like this. I envisioned him holding Matthew on his knee at the house and all of us laughing at "Chunk" – the nickname given to Matthew as a comparison of his birthweight to that of his one-pound siblings.

"AJ, I thought we were friends! Why are you telling people that I had no authority? You and I both know that I did, and I am in some serious trouble because of your lies?"

Getting the authority in writing from a Marine I would have taken a bullet for was not something that had ever crossed my mind. I simply trusted him – completely.

"Kelly, it's your ass or mine, and they're already gunning for you."

His simple admission is all I need.

Worth Dying For
L. Todd Kelly

He went on to explain that he knew his client had perjured himself in order to get through the *providency inquiry,* where each element of the offense is stated, including the *mens rea*, otherwise known as the state of mind.

He explained that he suborned the perjury because he didn't think he could win an actual acquittal, given that the pistol was found in the Sergeant's possession.

I now saw a man very differently than the one I thought I had known.

A MAN WHO ONCE HELD MY SON IN HIS LAP AS WE ATE DINNERS PREPARED IN MY HOME: A MAN I HAD JUDGED WORTH DYING FOR.

After every prosecutor and member of my defense team had spoken with the investigating officer and each one, to a person, had thrown me under the proverbial bus, the Colonel finally called me into the staff judge advocate's office to finalize the process of ending my career. I presumed that the SJA offered up her office to impress upon me the import of the meeting—as if I wasn't already convinced.

I was terrified that my career was about to be over (both as a Marine and as an attorney) and in disgrace. I started to think that perhaps my cavalier attitude towards sin and my turn from God was why I found myself in this place. Perhaps it was. Perhaps I needed to wake up!

Worth Dying For
L. Todd Kelly

After advising me of my right to remain silent under the UCMJ, the investigating officer informed me that things did not look good for me and that he was pretty sure there was not going to be much I could say to change things.

He just read my rights! Are they charging me with a crime, too?!

"I understand, sir," I almost whisper.

I could barely utter my next words, "I don't even know if this is legal, but I know it's the truth…"

I placed before him on the desk a recording device that had been hidden on top of my wall locker when I invited Captain Wiggins in to discuss his rationale for perpetuating this lie in my office. I hit the play button.

"You will be cleared of all wrongdoing, Captain."

"Thank you, sir."

But politics being what they were, I knew that the truth would not sway most people. Captain Wiggins was never prosecuted for his documented misconduct—a knowingly false accusation of a man who considered him a brother.

I doubt that AJ knows about that recording to this very day. I have to admit that until I was writing this book, a small part of me (a part that I am not proud of) hoped he would read this to feel the pain he inflicted.

However, God has freed me of that desire. As I write this now, because of His grace, I hope that if the man who was once my brother reads this—he will

Worth Dying For
L. Todd Kelly

know that, though it took me decades and several counseling sessions to forgive him.

I was re-assigned to serve as the Headquarters Battalion's executive officer—a billet to stash so that I couldn't cause any more trouble at the legal services center. I withdrew from the corporal's case to take the heat following me off my young client.

The Military Judge, Colonel William P. Hollerich, dubbed by those who practiced before him as "the screaming skull," heard my motion to recuse myself. Colonel Hollerich was intimidating to everyone who appeared before him—especially those of us who were significantly junior in rank.

Colonel Hollerich sat on the bench in his courtroom, a singularly ominous picture of military justice from my view from the counsel table.

"Are you certain, Captain Kelly?" Judge Hollerich asked me knowingly.

"No sir, I am not," I replied. "But I have a duty to my client that I took an oath to follow. The allegations against me center around this Marine's case and cannot help but hurt him."

As the words left my mouth, I worried that the following detailed defense counsel would *play the game*" at this young Marine corporal's expense. But…I convinced myself that I could no longer offer effective counsel.

Worth Dying For
L. Todd Kelly

"Your motion to recuse is granted, Captain."

I won.
It hurt.

Within a month, the corporal, a dedicated Marine who was not guilty of the crime he was charged with committing, entered a guilty plea to theft of a government weapon with my replacement defense counsel at his side. He received a Bad Conduct Discharge, reduction to Private, and six months confinement: the maximum sentence at a Special Court Martial. He lost all of his VA benefits.

Worth Dying For
L. Todd Kelly

FATHER'S LOVE. A Father's Love should never be for his job. This can be hard.

FATHER'S LIFE. A Father's Life is about his family – not his career.

FATHER'S FEAR. A Father's Fear must be managed to not change the nature of his relationship with his family.

FATHER'S FIGHT. A Father's Fight is to manage that fear.

FATHER'S WISDOM. A Father's Wisdom will permit him to manage fear while teaching his children the lessons they need without experiencing the uncertainties that he faces.

THE RETURN OF THE PATRIOT

16

RETURNING HOME

*Scarred and scorned, I'm
filled with hate.
The blame and treatment
that I ate,
Because I'd done what
they required,
And not the role I had
desired.*

*Just get me home, I want
to leave,
No longer to this band, I
cleave.
The Corps has hurt me; it
deceived,
It wasn't what I once
believed.*

*The irony was lost on me,
I wasn't still the same,
you see.
The lies that I believed
were true,
Hadn't I told others, too?*

*My wife had also trusted
me,
And I had not been true,
you see.*

*But that was not my
focus now,
I had to leave this Corps,
somehow.*

*Returning home by one
man's direction,
I thought it luck, for that
connection.
I took a job no one could
want,
Expecting that I'd hear
some taunt.*

*Reporting in I played my
role,
And honored those
placed in that hole.
The thanks and love their
families shared,
Reminding me of why I
cared.*

*The guns were fired, Taps
were played,
And on the ground, a
brother lay.
A brother for our nation
would die
A slow salute and Semper
Fi.*

•••••●●●•••

Worth Dying For
L. Todd Kelly

AT THIS POINT, I had become disenchanted with the United States Marine Corps. This, and the other miscarriages of justice, was born of a system set up to ensure convictions rather than justice were not what I signed up for. I loved this Corps. I loved the men and women I served with. Was it all a lie?

Marysue had been a *military brat* her entire life, but we chose, through many tears, to leave my beloved Corps—and the only way of life she had ever known. It was not what I had believed it to be. This was the last in a long line of nails in that coffin.

THIS CORPS WAS SIMPLY NO LONGER WORTH DYING FOR.

I received an unanticipated call at about 4:30 a.m., Hawaii time. Marysue's voice brought me, slowly, into full consciousness.

"Hello." She answered.

"No, he's asleep," she continued.

"I will tell him you called."

Though barely conscious., I asked, "Who was that?"

"Someone named General Composto called you."

"You just told the Staff Judge Advocate of the Marine Corps that I wasn't available?!"

I was WIDE AWAKE at that point!

Worth Dying For
L. Todd Kelly

I stammered in disbelief at this daughter of a Navy Captain who was my wife. *She knows better!* —I chose not to speak that thought.

General Composto thankfully laughed it off when I was finally able to speak with him.

"I understand you've had a tough time of it out there, Skipper?"

"Yes, sir," I explained the entire mess, or rather, messes.

With an almost fatherly kindness, he asked, "What can I do for you, Captain Kelly?"

"Sir, I am only licensed in Virginia, and my time in this gun club is over. I'd take ANY JOB in Virginia."

These are words that an experienced Captain of Marines knows better than to say. But I had no real choice.

My last nine months in the Corps were spent serving as the United States Marine Corps Casualty Officer. My primary job was to assist the families of Marines who had been killed with their benefits and last rights. As a collateral part of that duty, I knelt to hand flags to widows at Arlington National Cemetery in my dress blues.

The first time I donned my dress blues for a trip to Arlington was memorable, not because of who we were buried, but because of what the ceremony stood for. As the horse-drawn Caisson stopped and the pallbearers removed the flag-covered casket, I felt a

Worth Dying For
L. Todd Kelly

sense of pride for this Marine I never knew. I felt a sense of connection on a larger scale.

The slow cadence of that march and of the slowed salutes added to the sobriety of that moment. After I dropped my salute to the casket, the first volley of rifle shots almost scared me out of my position of attention. I held on and braced for the next two volleys.

Pride swelled with each one. Tears welled in my eyes as a lone bugler played "Taps" in the distance. I remembered why I first donned the uniform and what my oath had once meant to me. It began, again, to mean something.

As I took the carefully folded flag and turned to the widow, she seemed proud. As I took a knee, I noticed her tear. Then, I spoke the words I had been carefully rehearsing in my head:

"Ma'am, on behalf of a grateful nation, the United States Marine Corps, and the Commandant of the Marine Corps, please accept this token of our appreciation for the sacrifice your family has made for our freedoms."

PERHAPS, AFTER ALL, THIS NATION IS WORTH DYING FOR.

Worth Dying For
L. Todd Kelly

FATHER'S LOVE. A Father's Love can teach a wayward child that while some may have hurt him, it is not right to hold everyone else accountable.

FATHER'S LIFE. A Father's Life should be lived in honor to God, not to man's ways.

FATHER'S FEAR. A Father's Fear should not be of death but of dying without having demonstrated God's love.

FATHER'S FIGHT. A Father's Fight is to deny himself and live a Godly life.

FATHER'S WISDOM. A Father's Wisdom shows what is truly important in this life.

THE MORALITY OF MONEY

17

BABY LAWYER

"Baby Lawyer," what a term,
We want to shed it like some germ
That we have caught and cannot rid,
"I'm a lawyer – not a kid!"

But the term has meaning, there's no doubt,
When we first start, we have no clout.
As we are learning to find our voice,
Our clients have another choice.

They could choose a more seasoned speaker,
Rather than one whose voice is weaker.
Judges listen when hair turns gray,
It seems all wrong, but it is the way.

I've learned that money drives corporate greed,
And in its wake leaves those in need
It leaves them broken, dying, dead,
And some will turn to me instead.

Ego now turns into fear

As it is my voice, these people hear.
I am not sure if I can,
I want to help. Am I the man?

Learning of the money lust,
And that there is so little trust,
A younger lawyer's mind is set:
It's so much more than just a bet.

This "business" matters, and lives are changed,
But there are so many deranged
That convincing twelve that we are right,
Remains a monumental fight.

So now, for clients that I love,
And fear that there's no shortage of.
We take the fight to larger firms
And try to bring them to our terms.

It's not for greed, as many say,
But so that ours can see a day

Worth Dying For
L. Todd Kelly

When justice comes into their lives,
To be with husbands, kids, and wives.
The playing field is tilted down,

As we look up and all around,
Opponents and judges are all chatters
But we will fight for all that matters

••••••••••

IN MY EVENING HOURS, as I finished my time in the Corps, I sent a resume, law school transcript, and writing sample to every law firm in Virginia, it seemed. Each packet spiral was bound to stand out from the mass of applications that I knew were flooding these firms.

May 20, 1998. Ten years, ten months, and ten days. Discharged. Honorably. A Major in the United States Marine Corps Reserve. Still licensed to practice law.

A *Baby Lawyer* no more, I had to find my way as a civilian trial lawyer.

All those evening applications eventually resulted in a job offer. It was a pay cut from what a Marine Captain of my time-in-grade was making and far less than I would have made as a Major, but I was desperate to get on with this new career, and it was certainly more than an unemployed lawyer would make.

The *silk-stocking* law firm of Hunton & Williams interviewed me three times for one of their litigation teams. I wore my best suits and pretended to like sushi (it was a taste I would only later acquire and learn to appreciate all too well). When they decided to hire someone else, I was told my law school did not have

Worth Dying For
L. Todd Kelly

the *pedigree* they desired. I laughed at those *pedigrees* today, but it hurt at the time.

I found work as a plaintiff's personal injury trial lawyer in Newport News, Virginia. I didn't know that I had a penchant for this work yet. In my interview, I told Robert "Bobby" Hatten that I was never more alive than when speaking to a jury. He seemed to like that as an interview line, but I had no idea his plans for me were far from that vision.

The firm (at that time called Patten, Wornom & Watkins) made its name in the '80s, representing shipyard workers exposed to asbestos. These were hard-working men and women who had believed the lie told by Johns-Manville and other corporate entities that asbestos was safe.

Many of these hard-working men were dying from asbestos exposure, and even more were sick with cancers or other permanent illnesses caused by this airborne menace. Even their wives and closest family members were dying of the same diseases, inhaling the deadly silica when they dutifully cleaned their husband's clothing—shaking the invisible fibers of death into the air.

These jobs were never worth dying for, except for the corporate executives who didn't pay that price. These hard-working Americans' lives were simply a cost of business to the executives who cared more about bottom lines.

This reality was horrific enough. But the fact that Johns-Manville and the other manufacturers had actual

Worth Dying For
L. Todd Kelly

knowledge, based upon their own studies, that they were exposing people to deadly products instilled the passion to advocate for the injured people in me.

How could they?

How naïve I was to believe that morality even mattered to them.

Money is all they cared about.

I soon learned that this is just what big businesses do: make money regardless of who gets hurt. I distinctly remember one client with mesothelioma (a deadly cancer caused by one thing and one thing only: asbestos exposure).

This woman was too young to have worked in the shipyard before going to college and medical school.

THESE HARD-WORKING AMERICANS' LIVES WERE SIMPLY A COST OF BUSINESS TO THE EXECUTIVES WHO CARED MORE ABOUT BOTTOM LINES.

Her father, a pipefitter at Newport News Shipyard, had taken home scraps of the fireproof material to protect his young baby in her crib in case of a house fire. He was *protecting* her from the danger he was aware of, blind to the harm he was causing with the material he was handling.

As babies do, she would scratch at the material, making the friable asbestos airborne so that she would

Worth Dying For
L. Todd Kelly

inhale the nearly invisible particles. The disease, as it does, lay dormant in her lungs for almost thirty years—just long enough for the *infant* to graduate from medical school and begin her residency—before it reared its devastating impact.

Mesothelioma has a 100% success rate of killing its victims. But her daddy, arguably, got the worst of it—in a cruel twist of fate, he would live to watch his acts (intended to save his baby girl) kill his daughter painfully over the next two years. He would survive his own exposure.

Stories like these haunt trial lawyers. There may be those who can easily brush things like that off. Still, for most of us, the pain we feel, known as second-hand stress, creeps in like an invisible airborne particle that can devastate a life—one tragedy at a time for years until we succumb to the damage.

I KNOW THESE TRIAL LAWYERS: MEN AND WOMEN SCARRED BY THE PAIN INFLICTED BY UNCARING CORPORATIONS AND INSURANCE EXECUTIVES WHO CONSISTENTLY PLACE MONEY AHEAD OF HUMAN LIFE AND DIGNITY.

Some have simply called it *despair,* while others call it *second-hand PTSD*. Many have found their lives not worth living and sought relief from the stress and pain of these stories believing that the relief from that pain was worth dying for—and often intentionally—at their own hand.

Worth Dying For
L. Todd Kelly

After four years as an associate with the firm in Virginia (which later changed its name to Patten, Wornom, Hatten & Diamonstein), I determined (wrongly, as it turns out) that asbestos litigation was nearing its end. I also appeared to have hit a professional ceiling in my career at the firm. Not that it was a high ceiling, but the low pay of an associate was adding burdens on my marriage that were difficult to withstand.

When I asked for a raise, it was not greeted with welcome approval but with analogies to people with lots of marbles. The stress didn't remain at the office but came home, where the lack of income caused harsh discussions about who was contributing more to the marriage. I felt I had become merely a *wage-earned* in my home—and I was apparently not very good at that!

My decision to leave was hastened when Bobby Hatten asked me, in my annual review, how I felt about my work at the firm.

"We've had this discussion privately, Bobby. Why are you asking this in front of your partners?"

I pondered to myself. I answered his inquiry honestly: "I would prefer to be in the action in the courtroom, and while I respect the work of the men in this room who have done that work and laid the groundwork for so many to be compensated, my true calling is in the well of a courtroom."

In response to my honest recitation of where my heart lived, Alan Diamonstein, in his deep, slow, South Virginian drawl (born of his years in the Virginia

Worth Dying For
L. Todd Kelly

Legislature), was both flattering and ominous, as I knew it marked the end of my time at the firm: "Well, Todd, I expect nothing less from any self-respecting trial lawyer."

As those indelible words sunk in over the next few days, I made the decision to move to Pennsylvania (where I graduated from law school and where the prestige of The Dickinson School of Law was appreciated enough to help with job searching). I had gotten licensed there over the prior year.

This time, however, I fully understood that I could not work for forces that stood against individual people. I had to work for a plaintiff's firm. I had to help the injured—not the large corporations that injured people without regard for them, then make them fight for some small scrap of justice.

THESE CORPORATIONS FOUND MONEY WORTH EVERYONE ELSE DYING FOR.

Worth Dying For
L. Todd Kelly

FATHER'S LOVE. A Father's Love should place people ahead of profits. This can be challenging in a competitive industry.

FATHER'S LIFE. A Father's Life should exemplify the placement of priorities with people first.

FATHER'S FEAR. A Father's Fear must be managed so that the ultimate means of controlling that fear is in our Heavenly Father.

FATHER'S FIGHT. A Father's Fight is to protect his children, just as our Heavenly Father wants to protect us.

FATHER'S WISDOM. A Father's Wisdom is important to protecting his children. We do not have the wisdom our Heavenly Father has, but we must use what we have to its fullest.

Worth Dying For
L. Todd Kelly

CHILD-LIKE STUBBORNNESS

18

JESUS LOVES ME

Jesus loves me, this I know,
But I sure wish His face he'd show.
I haven't seen Him in so long,
I am weak – does He hear my song?

I'm a sinner, and I know that's true,
But You said that You'd love me, too.
If You love me, where are You?
Nothing I do reveals You.

If I read your word and pray,
You will listen, so You say.
If I call to you in pain,
You will hear me once again.
So, do You love me?
Say, do You love me?
Jesus, You love me?
The Bible tells me so.

I'm so busy, I can't stay,
I'm too busy to stop and pray,
I'm too busy now for You,
But there's still things that You should do...

Isn't that how this thing goes,
You grant wishes that I chose?
That must be there in your book
If I simply took the time to look.

• • • • • • • • • • • •

I KNOW THAT ONLY God completes me and that the only perfection I have ever experienced is watching His perfect love forgive me and welcome me home. For some reason, I keep finding a way to walk away from Him, only to hit my knees and crawl back eventually.

While working at Patten, Wornom, & Watkins, I started to attend Sunday morning services with Marysue and our three children at Hilton Christian Church in Newport News. It was an older church with

Worth Dying For
L. Todd Kelly

an aging congregation, but they welcomed our young family.

I was returning to a closer relationship with God and wanted Him in my life and my children's lives. The congregation was generally made up of shipyard workers and their families in the Hilton area of Newport News. Many of these people had been devastated by asbestos-related diseases that I saw in my professional life.

I recall a young doctor in her thirties who had just begun her career of helping others. When she was diagnosed with mesothelioma, we had to determine where her exposure had come from. Mesothelioma is a rare cancer caused by only one thing: asbestos exposure. It can sometimes lie dormant for up to fifty years but is always terminal, generally within two years, once it rears its head.

The only exposure we could find happened when she was an infant. Her father, a shipyard worker at Newport News Naval Shipyard, had brought home scraps of asbestos sheeting to line his baby's crib to save her life in the event of a house fire.

As babies do, this daughter would scratch at the sheeting, releasing the asbestos fibers into the air. She would then breathe those microscopic elements of death into her lungs. Because the body cannot remove these fibers, they rested there for over thirty years before the cancer was finally diagnosed.

It was sad to watch her demise. Watching her father, who was not ill, was devastating as he dealt with

Worth Dying For
L. Todd Kelly

the consequences of what he had unwittingly done. This was just one of many examples.

Our family's welcome at Hilton Christian Church was evident, and eventually, I was even asked to serve as a Deacon. I was honored to do this in this small Christ-centered church. My soul was enriched both at work and in my faith. I had been forgiven for the stray steps I had taken out of my marriage. I was, for a time, complete

But this was not my first attempt at a walk with God. While on active duty in the Marine Corps, I sporadically attended church services in the base chapel but didn't consider myself a regular attendee. I prayed —occasionally—but spent no time in His Word.

I again felt a strong connection to my Savior when I joined Hilton Christian Church. While I initially viewed these times as *walking* with God, in fairness, I wasn't mature enough to walk.

In truth, I'm merely crawling.

I struggled, professionally, with the cases that which these corporate giants had valued profits as worth dying for while simultaneously trying to reconnect with God.

Worth Dying For
L. Todd Kelly

FATHER'S LOVE. A Father's Love is unending, even when we walk away from it.

FATHER'S LIFE. A Father's Life is an example to his children, whether he wants it to be or not.

FATHER'S FEAR. A Father's Fear for his family's safety can only be controlled by a walk with God.

FATHER'S FIGHT. A Father's Fight is to protect his family while learning to rely upon God to protect the entire family, including him.

FATHER'S WISDOM. A Father's Wisdom will never be enough to walk without God.

Worth Dying For
L. Todd Kelly

COLD NIGHTS AND TEXAS CHARM

19

Pennsylvania

A hard, half-inflated mattress.
A cold, lonely night.
Clients demanding hours,
Don't understand the fight.

Friends try easing lonely,
And they invite me out for beers.
But that does not fill the empty,
It just postpones the fears.

This cannot be my calling,
This cannot be my end.
This place is cold and lonely,
But to the enemy, I won't bend.

Texas calls me home again,
And home again, I'll go.
I cannot wait to leave this place,
Cold, lonely—full of snow

•••••••••••

AFTER LEAVING THE FIRM, Patten, Wornom, Hatten & Diamonstein, I worked in Pennsylvania for just over a year for the law firm of Cohen & Feeley. I was a personal injury associate and was fortunate to work with a contemporary associate named Steven Margolis. Steve and I became good friends. He was Jewish, and we had discussions about our respective views on faith and the practice of law that were both intellectually challenging and stimulating. Steve's friendship helped me grow as an advocate and in my perspective of faith.

I could not sell the home in Virginia for almost a year, so I was forced to live away from Marysue and the kids.

During the week, I lived in a musty basement room that had been converted for the purpose by a retired Catholic Priest who lived upstairs in the main house.

Worth Dying For
L. Todd Kelly

This was all we could afford for me, given our situation. There was a bathroom in the basement, just down the hall from my room. Living in this one-room space was depressing in and of itself. I slept on an air mattress on the floor, which I re-inflated daily because it wouldn't hold air. There was no television. I frequently left this space unless I was sleeping. I did not like being there and resented not being in the nice home my wife and kids lived in.

I traveled to Virginia on the weekends to see them, but the six-hour drive got old. This weekend not in a position to take more.

Although I was working on some significant cases, my supervising attorney informed me that he determined that I was not ready to handle the actual trial on my own (even though I had worked them up to get them ready for trial and right up to the point that he took over the cases and settled them). The clients were well cared for. The partner who supervised me was well compensated, yet I continued to live in a basement apartment away from my family, driving twelve hours per week just to see my kids.

Ultimately, I remembered another lesson I learned in law school: my Texas-born body does not endure the cold well, and I did not like shoveling snow. Not at all. I decided to return to my native Texas in 2002.

I would only work for a plaintiff's personal injury law firm, helping injured people, so I sent resumes to personal injury firms in my home state, but few responses were forthcoming. Although I was becoming a seasoned associate, I was also a brand-new Texas lawyer.

Worth Dying For
L. Todd Kelly

My wife's sister and brother-in-law lived in Katy, a suburb of Houston, and she was pushing for me to look in that area. Then I received a call from Jacquelyn C. Gregan, a medical malpractice attorney at a boutique firm in Houston called Haskins & Gregan. She wanted to meet me, so I took some vacation time and flew down for the interview.

Jackie told me about how she started the Houston branch of an Arkansas law firm several years earlier when the firm's founder, John Haskins, retired. The existing version of the firm consisted of only Jackie, an associate, and their staff. She desperately needed another associate.

Jackie was charming and, in her own way, reminded me of my grandmother: warm and welcoming. She also expressed a desire to teach the medical aspects of the cases, so long as I was willing to put in the crazy hours. I was.

Working crazy hours was easy—that had always been my life. I accepted the offer on the spot. I had shoveled snow for the last time. Marysue and I loaded up the three kids and moved back to where I was always meant to be: Texas!

Worth Dying For
L. Todd Kelly

FATHER'S LOVE. A Father's Love pushes him to endure discomfort and sacrifice for his children.

FATHER'S LIFE. A Father's Life is about his family – not his own comforts, which must always come after he has taken care of his family.

FATHER'S FEAR. A Father's Fear of failure should not control his actions, but rather a faith in God that, as the ultimate Father, He will provide.

FATHER'S FIGHT. A Father's Fight is to take care of his family while trusting that God will carry the heavy burdens.

FATHER'S WISDOM. A Father's Wisdom will turn him toward God in his time of need.

Worth Dying For
L. Todd Kelly

THE ABANDONMENT OF OUR LIBERTIES

20

TEXAS JUSTICE

Justice seems so far away.
I tell those injured every day.
Texas voters just don't know
How far insurance lobbies go…

To cheat, lie, and conceal their aim:
To treat your loss of life – a game.
They dubbed us "greedy" who dared to fight –
And do not care what's wrong or right.

You believe what we know is false,
But it leaves so many at a loss.
That could be you – you don't believe
It must be a trick up my long sleeve.

This baby only wants a chance,
Not to run, or play, or dance.
That was taken on her birthday.
But those who did it will not pay.

You capped those losses with your vote.
Now they walk in here and gloat.
They know most of you will not believe,
So here they are: you to deceive.

If she is lucky, she may get a share
Enough to pay her doctor's care.
Her loss of innocence and life:
Not their problem. Not their strife.

The truth is that they skewed the laws.
Insurance money is the cause.
You believe that justice will cost you care,
But of that lie, you must beware.

Our leaders told you the doctors came.
Of course, they did – now we are lame.
"More doctors," they decried as laws were passed.
But do we want those - last in class?

Accountability – they escaped
But our people they have raped.

Worth Dying For
L. Todd Kelly

The flood that fled the other states,
Came where insurers and lawmakers mate.

The laws we passed brought more malpractice.
Still, doctors cry: "You must protect us."
The insurance lobby knows their craft.
Texans, they've given you the shaft!

Don't believe m—It won't matter.
Until your tears on my desk splatter,
As I explain, you have no case.

Then you'll finally see a trace

Of the evil lies that you have bought –
Too late: in that web, you are caught.
You'll hate me now that I've made clear
What up to now, you refused to hear.

But what if you had heard before?
Would you then storm out my door?
Or would you see this greedy soul
As one with justice as his goal?

• • • • • • • • • • • •

THE ASSOCIATE'S POSITION WITH Haskins & Gregan allowed me to represent victims of medical malpractice and nursing home neglect. I learned enough medicine (pulling many all-nighters in our medical library) to have some success in the courtrooms against doctors and nurses who had been inattentive or worse. I was shocked at the lack of care that I was learning exists!

I sued doctors trained to care for our most vulnerable newborns but ignored the apparent warning signs of fetal distress, leading to a lifetime of devastation for the child and the family. Most of these cerebral palsy cases could have been avoided if only these physicians had done their jobs and paid attention.

I worked with Patti Artavia, a funny and intelligent paralegal, who helped prepare my cases for trial. I learned as much from her as I did from Jackie, if not more.

Our investigative staff needed another investigator. Jackie's husband, Kevin, and her son, Matt, were not interested in the work anymore. My brother, Reagan, had complained about the auto parts retail industry for years. Pep Boys was just not fulfilling for him anymore. Perhaps he would take the job. Reagan jumped at the chance to change careers.

Within two years, the firm changed names: Haskins, Gregan & Kelly.

My name is on the door!

I've made it.

I witnessed insurance companies for these healthcare providers circle ranks and threatened expert witnesses that if they testified for an injured person, their own insurance would be terminated. This evident witness tampering was just par for the course. Our courts would not intervene, even when we presented clear evidence of it. How were we ever going to beat this?

Then came the *tort reform* legislative session of 2003 in Texas. The playing field would be tilted against injured Texans even more. Even if we were successful in court, there would be arbitrary *one-size-fits-all* caps on damages.

The Texas Legislature passed bills that further protected these doctors. I could not understand the level of hypocrisy in the bill, but I realized that speaking out for my clients would fall on deaf ears.

People would view me precisely as my entire profession had been labeled: a *greedy trial lawyer*.

> NOW, NO ONE WHO HAD THE INFORMATION NEEDED TO EXPOSE THE CORRUPTION OF THE SYSTEM COULD SPEAK WITHOUT CONFRONTING THAT CHALLENGE.

I soon realized that these lawmakers and the insurance companies working behind them were simultaneously evil but brilliant.

What about the Constitution?

> *"In Suits at common law, where the value in controversy shall exceed twenty dollars, the right of trial by jury shall be preserved, and no fact tried by a jury shall be otherwise re-examined in any Court of the United States, then according to the rules of the common law."*
>
> ~ 7th Amendment to the U.S. Constitution

How could the underlying belief that "The right of trial by jury shall be preserved" be preserved, if the jury awards an amount above the caps, that jury's verdict is reduced? Justice was not to be served. The *right to trial by jury* was not being preserved but rather undermined. The deterrent effect of our jury system was thwarted. So, what was I fighting for as a Marine? What is the point of fallen heroes if we just give away our rights?

I THOUGHT THESE WERE THE RIGHTS WE ALL AGREED WERE WORTH DYING FOR!

These were the rights that people before me fought so hard and died for.

The 7th Amendment promises that "no fact tried by a jury shall be otherwise re-examined in any Court of the United States," so legislators simply took it out of the court and stripped the jury of its power.

They completely ignored the preservation language.

Why would they do that?

Legislators who pushed for this *tort reform* talked about *frivolous* lawsuits but always failed to name one. They conveniently *forgot* that there were already laws in place to punish those who bring such suits.

They didn't *forget* at all. They just wholly failed to mention it.

They dub my brothers and sisters who would stand up for injured clients as *Greedy Trial Lawyers*; a moniker that flies in the face of economics.

THE LAW OF ECONOMICS, ON ITS VERY FACE, CAN CAUSE A PLAINTIFF'S ATTORNEY TO DECLINE TAKING ON A CASE WITH LITTLE CHANCE OF SUCCESS.

This is obvious when you consider that the Trial Lawyer will invest his money and time into the case and is only paid if he wins. What a foolish business model to begin with—and those who may be held accountable after that risk are assumed to want to convince the public that these well-educated professionals are so illogical as to take these enormous risks on frivolous cases? Though the truth is staring us straight in the face, the facts seem ignored, as name-calling is far more attractive to the general public.

As a partner at Haskins, Gregan & Kelly, I was proud of our work for so many victims of medical neglect and nursing home abuse, especially in light of the deck stacked against us. We knew these doctor and nurse defendants were not as saintly as their titles suggest. I was too proud to hold them to account. I completely forgot that God put me there.

Despite the public opinion about trial lawyers, our little firm was doing reasonably well for what it was. As a partner at the firm, I had finally found my footing and had reached a point where I felt comfortable enough— at long last—to build our family home. It was a large custom home in a beautiful, gated community on an acre and a half of land. We had designed our d*ream*, and I finally felt like I had *arrived*. I referred to this house as the one I built to die in. I could never have known how that dream would become a nightmare.

AT THE TIME, I HAD BUILT A LIFE I BELIEVED TO BE WORTH DYING FOR.

Worth Dying For
L. Todd Kelly

FATHER'S LOVE. A Father's Love must be for people, just as God commanded.

FATHER'S LIFE. A Father's Life is dedicated to serving others, as God commanded.

FATHER'S FEAR. A Father's Fear must be focused on other people, as we are commanded to care for them. Our fear should be in failing to provide that care.

FATHER'S FIGHT. A Father's Fight is against a world that does not care for people but for money, power, and other sinful pursuits.

FATHER'S WISDOM. A Father's Wisdom will show him which battles to fight and how to fight them for the betterment of other people.

THE TOXIC AMERICAN DREAM

21

Fair

Teach your children to be fair,
But is that what they'll see out there?
Teach equality in our courts,
Teach them fairness in our sports.

Fairness has but one abode,
The rest is just a simple ode.

We sing of justice and our rights,
Ignoring truth and all its plights.

The multitudes pay a price
So that the few can live so nice.
Be careful what you learn at school,
Or else you may be someone's fool

• • • • • • • • • • • •

MARYSUE AND THE KIDS were oblivious to the struggles of my work and what the work was doing in my head. While I was finally in a position to *provide* at a level I had always wanted, the weight of being the *breadwinner* was amplified by the fact that my wife's aging parents had moved in with us (they helped with the purchase of the home, and my need to overcome that contribution weighed on me daily). Life was good, but the pressure to provide more and more was building.

While things looked good from the outside, an undercurrent ran through our paradise. We had the house of our dreams, but I was stretched to the limit to pay for it. The kids were in private school, but I couldn't really afford that, either. As I worked longer and longer hours to afford the trappings of success, I became more and more bitter that I seemed to be in this struggle,

Worth Dying For
L. Todd Kelly

alone. Another income would sure help out. Socially, some of the neighbors were doctors, CEOs, and business owners. There was toxic talk and energy in the air about their disdain for trial lawyers—me. While we did make friends with some of the neighbors, others felt that the guy who notoriously sued doctors for a living simply didn't fit in. They looked upon me with disdain. This affected my kids: I recall Meghan coming home one day from school and innocently asking me, "Daddy, why do you hate doctors?"

"I don't, sweetheart," I replied, explaining my stance in a way my grade school daughter could comprehend.

"They should be held accountable when they do wrong—just like everybody else. Don't you?"

Was this accountability I was striving for in the medical profession worth the price I was paying?

**WAS IT
WORTH MY FAMILY DYING FOR?**

Worth Dying For
L. Todd Kelly

FATHER'S LOVE. A Father's Love should guide his children to the truth. Most importantly, to the truth that God is the only true justice.

FATHER'S LIFE. A Father's Life will impact his children at a very early age.

FATHER'S FEAR. A Father's Fear should be that his children are taught by those who do not know God or the truth.

FATHER'S FIGHT. A Father's Fight is to properly educate his children on the truth.

FATHER'S WISDOM. Father's Wisdom: A Father's Wisdom is gained from experiences that can be shared, but a part of that wisdom is in just how to share it.

SIN MULTIPLIED

22

DRINKING PAINS

The votes were cast without concern,
The Constitution may as well burn.
So many bought deceit and lies,
And do not seem to care who tries.

My very job has cast me in
A group they view as a liar's den.
I speak the truth; they will not hear
And all the while, destruction's near.

So, like the others, well-informed
I have, will drunkenness, adorned
A type of arrogance and pride,
Though that's not what I feel inside.

I drink to ease the constant pain,
That those who profit, whom I disdain,
Have won against those that they've harmed
And live their lives so wholly charmed.

••••••••••••

I WROTE AN OPINION piece in 2002 urging voters to avoid the mistakes we were making by changing the laws in Texas before we passed them. The voice of the Trial Lawyer fell on deaf ears. But, as Texans, we passed them anyway at the urging of our legislators (who had to sneak in a change to our Texas Constitution, eviscerating the *open courts* provision to that founding document to make it happen).

Those laws that tilted the scales even further away from justice for injured people took their toll on my partner and me—as if they weren't already tilted enough!

Worth Dying For
L. Todd Kelly

In the wake of destroying our legal protections, Jackie drank a lot. The stress for her was starting to overtake her as she began to come to work in gym clothes.

She would claim she was *working out*, which explained why she never had her water bottle. I was impressed with her dedication until Patti alerted me that that wasn't water in that bottle.

Jackie was not alone in trying to escape the pain caused by these laws that blocked our efforts to help innocent children and defenseless elderly abuse victims. A martini at lunch turned into two, three...or even four. This became our team's routine to ease the Stress.

Sitting at the Fox and Hound one afternoon in 2004, Jackie and I were drinking our lunch, as usual, when a female associate joined us. She had become a regular, too. Feeling too intoxicated on much less alcohol than normal, I found myself entangled with my associate back at the office, where we were nearly caught in the act on the firm's conference table in what should have been a far more embarrassing situation than it ended up being.

I knew then that things had gone too far and had to end. The next day, I offered to resign. Jackie was disappointed but asked me not to leave. So, I stayed, and having already crossed the line, the associate and I continued our affair.

Between days in the bar and office rendezvous, my reckless behavior only worsened.

Worth Dying For
L. Todd Kelly

IT WASN'T LONG BEFORE THE DRINKING CAUSED ME TO SERIOUSLY CONSIDER MY REALITY (AND MORTALITY) AS I CONTINUED TO VEER EVER CLOSER TO IMPENDING DOOM.

Driving home from the Fox and Hound after too many drinks led to several close calls with the concrete median on Beltway 8. On one such occasion, I was determined to see my little girl cheer for her team at Fort Bend Baptist Academy (a private school I couldn't afford). I somehow managed to show up in the stands.

My state of intoxication, however, made me far from welcome. My loud, obnoxious rooting and hollering caused such an unacceptable display that Marysue informed me that I had embarrassed my daughter (and the entire family) and that they never wanted me to go to another game.

These moments of stupidity, together with too many hours that I will never remember, helped me to determine that I didn't want to die in a drunken car crash or continue to disgrace my children.

My life was worth living—even if not for me.

THAT ESCAPISM WAS NOT WORTH DYING FOR.

Worth Dying For
L. Todd Kelly

FATHER'S LOVE. A Father's Love should focus on his family over the pressures of this world.

FATHER'S LIFE. A Father's Life is about family, so don't throw it away over things out of your control.

FATHER'S FEAR. A Father's Fear of external forces is to be given to God, who provides. This must remain in focus.

FATHER'S FIGHT. A Father's Fight is with his own pride. He must realize who is in control.

FATHER'S WISDOM. A Father's Wisdom will guide him to seek God when things do not go well—rather than worldly relief.

Worth Dying For
L. Todd Kelly

FROM ONE ADDICTION TO ANOTHER

23

THE ANTI-DRUG

Though alcohol relieves some pain,
It finds its way back in again.
And the pain I cause under its spell,
Increases pain and empowers hell.

It must be somewhere else I turn
To find relief from anger's burn
I learn to kick, to punch with my palm,
I learn to fight, but more – to calm.

My sons are with me in this class,
We are learning this art fast.
The time I spend with each of them
Is like repairing a long-torn hem.

So to this art, I start to cleave,
And never, it seems, want to leave.
But soon, it, too, starts to take hold
And leaves my home alone and cold.

••••••••••••

I STARTED SEEING how far I had fallen and was determined to reshape my life. My boys started taking Karate at a local Karate dojo. I decided to join them and purchased my first gi or karate uniform. Zen-Do Kai Karate became my anti-drug, and I loved it.

This situation was perfect, and fortunately my *senseis* (instructors), Shawn and Sean, whose names often caused some confusion about exactly which one we were talking about, quickly became some of my closest friends. As it turned out, Shawn's fiancé, Heidi, was an attorney who was unhappy at her current firm, which made her a perfect new hire to come to work with me and Jackie.

Worth Dying For
L. Todd Kelly

Our friendships blossomed from there, and there was rarely a weekend that we didn't spend together. Heidi would frequently ask me, "What are we doing this weekend," as if getting together was a foregone conclusion. The questions were just "Where?" and "When?" We all showed up.

I practically lived at the dojo when I wasn't at the office. While it was a great escape from the stress and the booze. It soon became apparent that this anti-drug, too, was widening the rift in my marriage. Marysue and I rarely went to bed simultaneously, and intimacy simply wasn't. She knew about most of my affairs, and an intimate relationship with her cheating husband was not at the forefront of her mind. We were both becoming very alone. Once her source of love and companionship, I was now the person she came to when she wanted to go the salon or buy Meghan a new purse—if she came to me.

I was, at least, successful in my karate training. With that training, my excessive drinking came to an end. I was moving through the ranks with my boys and enjoying this particular time with them. I watched them grow and progress into young men and I could not have been prouder.

Shawn was the consummate martial artist. He had been training since he was nine years old. He had tremendous talent and was great with kids; short in stature, with a shaved head, Sean was a typical jokester who kept a sense of humor about everything he did. Karate, however, was his passion.

Sean, on the other hand, was quiet. He was a little larger than Shawn and prided himself not on speed and agility like his counterpart but on being highly technical in the art. He was the perfect complement to his brother.

These two took their belt tests together for every belt since they were red belts. They complemented each other perfectly, and they were best friends.

Worth Dying For
L. Todd Kelly

FATHER'S LOVE. A Father's Love should encourage quality time with his children.

FATHER'S LIFE. A Father's Life is about family, so he must not lose focus of the purpose behind his actions.

FATHER'S FEAR. A Father's Fear should focus on the eternal consequences of his actions rather than the temporal ones.

FATHER'S FIGHT. A Father's Fight ensures that his children are taught to be calm in their own storms and seek God, who can handle their temporary battles.

FATHER'S WISDOM. A Father's Wisdom must be shared with his children to point them to God.

Worth Dying For
L. Todd Kelly

RACING INTO THE BRICK WALL

24

Too Good for That

Sitting on the hill, I built,
Insulated from turmoil and tilt.
I fear for others for whom I care,
I don't see the dragon lying there.

Sitting in my own despair,
The depth of this reclining chair.

I will not give away my pride,
Not for my kids, my home, my bride.

I won't do that, I oft declare.
But my failures now they all will share.
Perhaps just a new career,
"I will not work" is all they hear.

••••••••••••

BACK AT THE OFFICE, Jackie's downward spiral only worsened. Her trajectory finally came to fruition in a trial in Beaumont.

She asked me to go with her, even though I had not been mainly involved in the case until then. I watched her as she struggled to comprehend the witnesses' answers and was unable to form coherent questions on cross-examination. She was as sober as sober got for her then, but she was incomprehensible.

I knew she had given everything she had to this profession—her youth, physical health, and even her mental health. I knew that her prime was over. It scared me.

I was already running the day-to-day functions of the office, given my partner's excessive absences and

Worth Dying For
L. Todd Kelly

drunkenness. She seemed intent on this downward spiral that would surely kill her.

Is it worth it? I wondered.
Is this a life even worth living?

Jackie knew that I was disappointed in how she handled the stress of the career we chose and the strain of being unable to help people as we once did. It was clear that I had simply become a daily reminder to her of what she was supposed to be, even if I was far less than the perfect image of that ideal.

Eventually, Patti, Heidi, Reagan, and I were the only ones performing and supporting this slowly dying law firm. It was a lot of weight for four people to hold that of ten. Try as we did to save it, we soon realized we were carrying too much. We had serious discussions about breaking out on our own but worried about surviving the economic downturn caused by *tort reform*. The question loomed, "How would we be able to help our clients now?"

We also worried about what would happen to our new, young associate, Heidi. She was the latest addition to a firm struggling with the weight of significant expenses and new, restrictive laws that deprived our clients of a true jury verdict and depriving us of the ability to make a living. It was clear that she was going to be let go any day. I worried for her and how she'd make a living, especially because she was about to be married to a karate instructor.

It seemed all the parts of my little world were somehow interconnected. Marysue, the kids, and I looked forward to weekends with our friends Heidi

Worth Dying For
L. Todd Kelly

and Shawn. I did not want to see them hurt by what I knew was likely coming.

I knew that jobs were hard to find for young lawyers, but I had room in my home for Heidi and Shawn to live until they got back on their feet. So I told them I had them covered when that time finally came. It wasn't going to be too different from our weekends together anyway.

I did not expect what came next.

After one of her ever-more-frequent alcohol-infused lunches with her husband Kevin, Jackie, came into my office and closed the door.

Here it comes, I thought.

Will she make me fire Heidi?

"I have decided that we can no longer afford you," were her words.

My skin turned cold. I couldn't move my body, as the oxygen seemed drained. I did not see that coming. After all, I'd been running this firm while she drank and smoked marijuana in her office. How would this firm survive without someone sober enough to run it?

"Can you give me a minute to gain my composure?"

"Sure."

For the first time since I was fifteen, I had no job—and no prospects. Not to mention that I had been fired for the first time.

Worth Dying For
L. Todd Kelly

Marysue's disdain for me at being fired could not be disguised. It was clear that she had lost all respect for the man she once loved, and it was clear that she was right—to a point.

"Just take any job you can find!" she urged. "A real man supports his family." Her words cut deeply.

"I'm a trial lawyer!" I demanded, desperately trying to hold on to the identity I had given myself. "I'd rather cut grass than work for a defense firm!"

Amid my financial desperation and Marysue's urging, I bit the bullet and interviewed with an insurance defense firm. They were a captive counsel firm for Zurich, North America. The interview went well, and they expressed interest. I needed a long, hot shower when I walked out. I would truly rather cut grass.

"I can't work for those people," I told Marysue when I returned home. "I meant it when I said I would rather cut grass."

But, on the brink of bankruptcy and home foreclosure, with three kids and a wife to support, Marysue was not happy with my response. I was already taking an unemployment check just to feed the family. No one, it seemed, was hiring.

I had considered using what little savings we had to buy a koi pond building company and just build koi ponds and teach karate. I liked the idea of this simple life (sort of like Mr. Miagi from *The Karate Kid*), but it was not well received at home.

Worth Dying For
L. Todd Kelly

Is this what I have become?
Good lawyers don't live like this, do they?

IS THIS THE JUSTICE THAT I HAD ONCE BELIEVED WAS WORTH DYING FOR?

Worth Dying For
L. Todd Kelly

FATHER'S LOVE. A Father's Love will cause him to do things for his family that he would not otherwise choose to do.

FATHER'S LIFE. A Father's Life is not his own, so pride has no place in his decisions, which will affect his family.

FATHER'S FEAR. A Father's Fear about career choices must be given to God, who provides. This must remain in focus.

FATHER'S FIGHT. A Father's Fight is with his own selfish pride. He must provide a nurturing environment, even when things are not what he wants.

FATHER'S WISDOM. A Father's Wisdom comes from God and must turn to Him in those times of need.

Worth Dying For
L. Todd Kelly

THE TRUE HEART OF A (GOOD) TRIAL LAWYER

25

READY

The room is empty, not a sound.
The air is still, and all around—
The silence, I know, will not last
For the fight is clear and long since cast.

The strain I wear upon my face,
The fright I've had of this cold place,
Will they see the fear in me?
Or will I hide it so they see…

Something more than what I feel.
Something more akin to steel?
Can I stand with them in the courtroom's well,
Or is this armor just a shell?

Will my words betray my fear?
Or will I speak and make it clear
That justice demands they bend an ear
And send a message all will hear?

The boxes filled with words I've honed
The arguments that I have owned.
But now the other ones arrive—
It seems the enemy is alive.

I count their boxes one by one
The number now has me undone.
What could those boxes be about?
Twice the number; twice the clout?
I try to calm, relax my wit:
The number won't determine it.
I smile, shake hands. I hate that ass!
I wish these pleasantries would pass.

"Counsel, are you ready to proceed?"
Thank God, the judge—that's all I need.
I hear his words; my hands grow steady—
"Yes, your honor, the Plaintiff's ready."
"Ready"

•••••••••••

Worth Dying For
L. Todd Kelly

I WAS STRUGGLING. My family watched it. My kids watched it. I was desperate. I was also ashamed. I had no job, and I didn't have any prospects to even offer a sense of hope to my family for recovery from my undoing. It was challenging to find the motivation to wake up in the morning with no job to go to, so I sent resumes from my home office, hoping each time I hit *return* that the bad luck streak I had been on would find its end.

I had never met Steve Davis or JD Davis, both of the Davis & Davis Law Firm in Houston before I became jobless. Though they shared the same name (and the same desk), these men are not brothers (Well, they are in Christ). They responded to one of my resumes and invited me to meet with them.

When I went to their office to meet with them, Davis did not have a job for me. They simply wanted to help me. After all, the heart of a trial lawyer is to help others, and these men were true trial lawyers with big, open hearts. Aside from a job, I didn't even know how they could have known what I needed.

They introduced me to a children's book I'd never read, entitled *Who Moved My Cheese*. It was an appropriate choice for changing my troubled mindset, as my *cheese* had indeed been moved.

Now—where did it go?

That is the question!

Understanding that watching me in my current desperate situation was probably not the healthiest environment for my children, Davis offered to let me use a desk and an empty office in their suite. At the same time, I diligently searched for something more permanent.

This is what I wish people would see when they think of Trial Lawyers instead of what's deliberately portrayed by our adversaries—whom we work to hold accountable in courts of law for their own true misdeeds.

> THIS IS THE LEVEL OF CARING THAT MAKES US WHO WE ARE. BUT IT'S ALSO WHAT MAKES US VULNERABLE.

I contacted another trial lawyer, Andy Vickery, of Vickery & Waldner. When I *interviewed* Andy, he explained the office-sharing arrangement he had entered with others in the office and showed me the empty office at the end of the hall, where he suggested I move into practice. His partner, Paul Waldner, referred to that office as "the end of the duodenum."

As I left Andy Vickery's office at One Riverway that day and stepped into the parking garage, I stopped and looked toward Heaven, "Okay, God, I hear you. I'll do it."

At that moment, with no plan to open my own law firm, The Kelly Law Firm, P.C. was born. The ultimate pinnacle I then believed to be worth devoting my life to.

Worth Dying For
L. Todd Kelly

FATHER'S LOVE. A Father's Love provides what His children need when they need it.

FATHER'S LIFE. A Father's Life is an example for his family and other fathers.

FATHER'S FEAR. A Father's Fear is normal and is understood by others who have faced it. It can be dealt with in healthy ways by turning to others when the need arises.

FATHER'S FIGHT. A Father's Fight is letting go of his will and allowing others to help. This is not weakness, but acceptance of who is in control.

FATHER'S WISDOM. A Father's Wisdom will allow him to accept the help he needs so that his children do not suffer.

Worth Dying For
L. Todd Kelly

SECRETS, SEX, AND LOTS OF SUCCESS (OR SO I THOUGHT)

26

GOOD TO BE THE KING

To be "the king," they say, is good.
To climb as high as any could.
And sitting there from this high view,
I think I start believing, too.

What's not to like about this spot?
But it's the web, and I've been caught.

I feel the need to feed this beast,
Or I will fall back to my least.

The price is small, it's just my time.
There's plenty more, and it's no crime.
I work until I'm not awake,
It's just the "Daddy Time" I take.

•••••••••••

ALTHOUGH I HAD not planned to open my own law firm, this was the chance to do it right—to focus on cases that moved me emotionally and to make a difference in the world.

All I needed now was to find someone to give me a business loan. I could hire Patti and rebuild my team if I could manage that. I honestly didn't think I could do this without her. But the loan was a challenge, as I had no cases. Oh, and I was broke! I did, however, have one commodity: my reputation for hard work and results.

I hoped that Heidi and Reagan would join me as soon as I could find a way to pay them a salary.

Fortune smiled when a banker friend, who had funded some cases for me while working with Jackie, agreed to go out on a limb based on my history with him. He authorized a $60,000 small business loan,

Worth Dying For
L. Todd Kelly

which, though not enough to pay me and Patti, was enough to bring Patti on board if I didn't take a paycheck. So that's what I did. This was my turn to make things right and I knew I could run this firm better than Jackie!

Cases came. There were many people getting hurt out there by others who just didn't care enough to put safety first. During my first six months of business, a lawyer who was a few years behind me at Dickinson and who practiced in Washington, DC, referred a case to me that would change everything: Jamie Leigh Jones, a young military contractor who had reportedly been gang-raped in Iraq by military contractors, then locked in a shipping container when she had the audacity to report what had happened to her.

The signing of that high-profile case led to a funding company offering to pay off my existing loan and gave my firm additional funding. The first one-million-dollar line of credit allowed me to bring Heidi and Reagan over. As the cases got better, we grew. We grew quickly.

The Kelly Law Firm had a great run for a while. We generated a fair amount of business through our individual reputations, word of mouth, and the tremendous free press we were getting on the military contractor sexual assault cases.

We created and maintained a professional multimedia presence that touted our professional accomplishments. The team grew to eight lawyers and a strong, seasoned legal staff. We even opened a second office with a national presence through numerous *counsel* relationships with firms nationwide. We were doing great things! Students from local law schools wanted to intern in the law firm I had created—just for the experience. I hired several—or I let them work there.

As my firm grew and progressed, so did my martial arts ability and presence. I became a black belt in karate under Shawn and his Sensei, Robert Gifford, at Safety America. Along with my promotion to black belt, I was asked to take over the operation and ownership of the karate school. This happened within months of opening my firm. It would take more time away from home, but I rationalized that I could train with the boys in the evenings. I rebranded this Safety America branch location into Lone Star Karate & Self-Defense.

FATHER'S LOVE. A Father's Love cannot be for his profession but is an alluring trap.

FATHER'S LIFE. A Father's Life is about family, so don't focus too much on career goals.

FATHER'S FEAR. A Father's Fear of financial ruin can take him away from the primary role he is to serve if he is not careful.

FATHER'S FIGHT. A Father's Fight is with his own pride. He will never be *The King*, as that role is taken by an Almighty King who loves us all.

FATHER'S WISDOM. A Father's Wisdom will remind him of his role as a father and servant.

Worth Dying For
L. Todd Kelly

THE DIRTY LITTLE SECRETS ABOUT MILITARY CONTRACTORS

27

THE SPARK

She wanted only to be free
From lecherous men at home.
She took with her the dream she had,
That she was not alone.

She believed she was a part,
Of a team of righteous men.
But that belief would lead her down
A road that others had been.

Just a girl, she signed away
Her right to jury trial.
Not known to her but to the men…
She'd face harm in a short while.

She tried to make some friends, you see
On that fateful summer day.
They drugged her, then each took their turn,
As if in some sort of play.

They drugged her as they passed a drink
She took in naïve trust.
They watched her consciousness recede
And then appeased their lust.

Lust for sex or power—so
It really matters not.
It only mattered to them then
That they knew they'd not be caught.

They never thought they'd pay a price:
They never had before.
She was not treated as their friend,
They raped her, and what's more:

They tore her body as they laughed
And really didn't care.
They knew her story'd never pass,
So her body they would share.

They'd never paid a price before
For doing evil things.
Military contractors
Ignored these evil rings.

Profits depended first, you see
Upon the public's view.
It serves their greedy means therefore
For justice to be skewed.

Worth Dying For
L. Todd Kelly

They force those suffering before
Who had the nerve to tell
Into secret "resolution"—
And thus, a silent Hell.

Call it quick, quiet, easy—see
Just like the Star Chamber
Arbitration, DRP
Just keep a lid on her!

That's how the royal "nobles"
In England's tyranny of Olde
Kept rule over the lowly serfs,
And history has told…

That the founding fathers of our land
Despised this power, greed, and might.
They chose to have no part in these
So they wrote a Bill of Rights.

Keep the secret in the dark,
Don't let the public see.
But this one chose to be the spark,
We wish we all could be.

Refusing to accept that this
Was "related" to her job,
She took her fight to the courts
And stirred an angry mob.

Her fight was won in courts, and then
On appeal and more.
Congress took an interest in
What happened off our shore.

She changed the law for others too,
Raped, assaulted, and harassed.
Because her heart and cause were true,
Better laws were passed.

But her employer still refused
To admit complicity
In the evil that misshaped her body
And stirred this swarm of bees.

So off to trial, she had to go
To make them answer for
All the things they did to her
And the women raped before.

As we consider who is right,
Which way those scales should tilt—

Worth Dying For
L. Todd Kelly

I have to ask you, isn't this
Why courtrooms first were built?

They painted her story as
One built on greed and lies.
Their money bought a verdict,
But that's no great surprise.

At least when she lies down at night
Jamie knows the truth:
They had to fight with all their might,
To keep justice from this youth.

•••••••••••

THE JAMIE LEIGH JONES case put us on the map at the firm. Jamie and I were interviewed by 20/20's Brian Ross and featured on that television news program along with other victims of sexual abuse by military contractors.

We were also featured on both the Rachael Maddow Show and on MSNBC. Her story, and our fight for justice, were featured as one of the four cases detailed in the documentary film, *Hot Coffee, the Movie*.

As media hype and controversy around her case heated up, Jamie and I were invited to Washington, DC, to speak to legislators about the evils of pre-dispute, mandatory, binding, secret arbitration—especially as it applied to military contractors overseas.

Some federal laws were changed. Arbitration was defeated (at least temporarily) in the narrow context of military contractors involved in sexual assault allegations. I took enormous pride in my team's efforts to assist in this corporate giant's arbitration clause being struck down for the first time in its history.

Worth Dying For
L. Todd Kelly

Jon Stewart did a segment referring to legislation around Jamie's case on *The Daily Show*, entitled "Rape Nuts." That is when my son, Josh, recognized that his dad was up to something big—when Jon Stewart talked about it.

Local news programs picked us up on numerous occasions.

Prospective clients were calling around the clock!

Jamie and I were recognized for our efforts by the American Association for Justice, where she was awarded the Making a Difference Award and where I was invited to speak on the struggles of navigating her case. We were also invited to present her story to law schools, including the University of Texas. The National Employment Lawyers' Association asked us to come and present her story at their annual conference.

I started believing in my own press. Nice things get written when you're winning. I took it all in and savored all the glory as if it were all according to my own plan.

I HAD STARTED TO BELIEVE THAT I DID THIS MYSELF. TO MY SHAME, I HAD FORGOTTEN THE ONE WHO GAVE ME THIS CHANCE—MY SAVIOR, MY GOD. *JESUS, I AM SORRY.*

Despite the improvements in my public image, my life at home was falling apart. Between karate and a crazy travel and work schedule, I was rarely home; when I was home, there was only arguing. Marysue had

Worth Dying For
L. Todd Kelly

lost all trust in me, and rightfully so. I had proven too many times that my confidence came from the attention of women because I took that attention wherever I could, and I traveled out of town often.

Marysue demanded more of my time, but time was a commodity I simply didn't have. I struggled to keep things afloat, and she was uninterested in my work. I couldn't focus on our *parenting methods* or our *time together* when I had a case demanding that I constantly give every ounce of my being to it. My standard response was, "I cannot do that now—Jamie needs me."

As the case progressed, even more of my attention was demanded by things other than my family. Mysterious things happened during Jamie's case against Halliburton and KBR. One witness mysteriously drove off a road in California to her death. A local court reporter, with whom I had become friends over the years, died in her kitchen with the transcript of the deposition of the alleged rapist still in the process of being transcribed on her computer.

There were also other mysterious happenings. Coincidence? Perhaps.

At some point, I called a meeting of my firm to discuss the literal risks of taking on the world's largest military contractor. As I sat at the conference room table, I looked each dedicated team member in the eye.

"I don't know exactly what we are up against or if we're truly in danger, but if you do not want to stay, I understand. I'll write you letters of recommendation and help you find other jobs." I told them. "I have

Worth Dying For
L. Todd Kelly

decided that The Kelly Law Firm will pursue justice for Jamie Jones regardless of risk."

I had decided that this cause may have been the very reason for my life. If it costs that, then so be it. My brave team agreed. Not one person left. The level of courage represented by my team was evident: This case and everything it stood for was worth the risk to everyone. Reflecting on it, I would be credited with the courage—but the team that held me up was filled with that quality.

While fighting Jamie's case under public scrutiny, I was also involved in a toxic tort chemical case that took equal time and far more financial investment from my firm. My financial backers encouraged relationships I would never have been a part of except for the pressure from folks with their hands around the neck of my money bags.

I became involved with lawyers who did not have the same client-centered focus I had seen in other trial lawyers. These lawyers were not typically lawyers for people (Trial Lawyers). They were, I would learn, in it *only for the money*.

The firm borrowed over $30 million to fund the litigation against BNSF Railroad for dumping creosote all over Somerville, Texas. While the lawyers who brought us into the case were not my type of people, the cause was just. Creosote, the material used to coat railroad ties, had been dumped in the lake, buried in the ground, and burned, so that it permeated the air over this pretty little Texas town for decades. People in Somerville, Texas, were born with birth defects at an alarming rate and dying in their early 50s of cancers rarely seen in people that young. But they didn't realize what was killing and maiming them.

I didn't try these cases because of my focus on the Jones case, but I had partnered with lawyers I trusted. The lawyers who encouraged my involvement convinced me they would succeed and improve my financial situation. Given my other commitments, I decided that this one had to be just a business deal. So I kept my focus on Jamie. That's how I had to view it.

My line of credit, however, had gotten out of hand due to the funding of the Somerville litigation. It seemed that my firm was now on very shaky financial ground. I borrowed millions of additional dollars to support the Somerville litigation and the other cases in which the firm was involved. I had become utterly dependent on the lenders.

> IN MY NAIVETÉ I DIDN'T REALIZE THOSE BORROWED FUNDS WERE PART OF A PONZI SCHEME DISGUISED AS A LENDING INSTITUTION.

The trial team lost the first of the Somerville cases. I didn't have time to take that on personally, so I withdrew and cut substantial losses before they got worse. If I was to have any chance of saving my law firm, I had to focus. I was now personally in debt to the Ponzi-scheme lenders for over $12 Million. I was, once again, at the end of my professional rope… unless I could bring justice to Jamie Leigh Jones.

Worth Dying For
L. Todd Kelly

I knew that Jamie's case was righteous and worth my sacrifice, and I had put all of my trust and hope in my belief that the jury would eventually see the truth and do the *right thing* if I could just get it to a trial.

There was an arbitration provision in Jamie's employment contract, and the military contractor wanted to compel her case into binding, secret, unappealable arbitration (known in the industry as the place where cases go to die). Arbitration is one-sided, secret, and full of reasons why the *little guy* will never have a fair shot against a large corporate entity, so I fought arbitration at all costs.

Against all odds, we beat Halliburton's forced, secret, pre-dispute, binding arbitration provision at the trial court level. We even held on to the 5th Circuit Court of Appeals ruling.

We would get a trial unless the Supreme Court took it away!

THIS GIRL AND HER CAUSE, THAT I RISKED MY FIRM, MY LIFE, AND MY FAMILY FOR, WAS—I BELIEVED WORTH DYING FOR.

Worth Dying For
L. Todd Kelly

FATHER'S LOVE. A Father's Love cannot be about fame and popularity if he is to be a good father.

FATHER'S LIFE. A Father's Life needs to center on his children. Good works are fine, but when they become the primary focus, they are no longer *good*.

FATHER'S FEAR. A Father's Fear should be centered on his children and the example he sets for them rather than on an image he tries to build.

FATHER'S FIGHT. A Father's Fight is to recognize those things that he can control and those that he cannot.

FATHER'S WISDOM. A Father's Wisdom will keep him in God's word when the world tries to pull him away.

YOU CAN'T OUTRUN THE DEVIL

28

THE GREEDY PLAINTIFF

You hate my "greedy" clients, but I hope that you will hear
That when I see the devastation to those that you hold dear
I tell them how you feel and that their damages are naught
Because it doesn't matter right or wrong—as once we all were taught.

They tell me, one and all, how their case is not "the same."
For they have never been involved in this litigation game.
Their damages are real, they urge, and their cause of action just—
Unlike my "other" clients— who just chase their money lust.

As they unfold to me their story, "I am different," they all claim
Though every time I hear it, it is hauntingly the same.
They voted for the laws now used to minimize their right
In favor of a corporate interest—so it could flex its might.

Those with money bought the power and the politicians too.
Justice cost them money, and the wealthy clearly knew
That protecting ill-gained profits means to take— but not to pay
Even when they harmed us all—if blame they could defray.

Now armed with only me, and the system that they scorned
These "different" injured people see the lies that they adorned.
They now see how the wealthy corporate entities deceived—
Far from paying for the harm they caused, they now will be relieved.

They bought the laws our Founders meant to equalize us all.
It didn't take a battle— not one of them did fall.
They simply used their money, power, might mixed in with greed
To convince you all that these protective laws were not a need.

Worth Dying For
L. Todd Kelly

Justice will not find its way to help your loved ones now.
You scorned and mocked me all those years, as I tried to tell you how.
I'm sorry, truly, that the corporate lies that you have bought.
Now find you broken, bankrupt, in the web in which you're caught.

I used to think it justice when those who voted out their right
Were forced to fight an enemy with money, and its might.
But now I just feel sorry—for the people didn't know,
And they go home defeated. But the bottom lines still grow.

So heed my tearful warning, all of you who might be harmed.
If you by corporation's greed, have been so wholly charmed.
Do you really think they'll help you when they cause you death or pain,
Or will your pleas for justice, like the "others," meet disdain?

If you think that you are different than those they've harmed before:
Those who needed help to cross the threshold of my door,
I hope you never have to learn the hard and awful truth:
That justice for so many is a dream that died with youth.

But the dream was not allowed a peaceful way to die
My brother and sister warriors have held this battle cry.
You do not listen, do not care, until it strikes your home
And once it does it's far too late—now with us you will roam.

But labeled "Greedy Plaintiff" with your "frivolous lawsuit,"
No one cares to hear about your aimless, "lottery" pursuit.
The Trial Lawyer that you hired will do his best to sway,
But it would have been much better if you'd listened yesterday.

Worth Dying For
L. Todd Kelly

SUITE 1100 AT One Riverway in Houston, Texas, was a showpiece of an office. Sitting on the eleventh floor of this sky-rise in Houston's Galleria area, our office space housed five law firms who worked together in a collaborative effort as *Justice Seekers*. The firm logos were etched into the glass doors at the front of our suite. It had the look and feel of a distinguished, successful law firm. The tenants in the suite often worked out the details of our cases in the office smack courtroom (a sign of our self-perceived importance), as we prepared our clients and ourselves for the battle that is a trial.

These brother and sister Trial Lawyers introduced me to the exceptional methods of trial presentation taught at the Trial Lawyers' College (TLC.) Most notably, my close friends, Ron Estefan and Andy Rubenstein, taught me how to use these techniques to connect on a deeper level with my clients as I learned to *walk a mile in their shoes*.

I first applied to the Trial Lawyers' College in 2007 and was disappointed when I was not accepted into that class. I would try and fail again in 2008 despite assurances that I'd be accepted. However, I was privileged to work with masters of the technique in our suite for those years before I finally got the call to attend the three-week course in Dubois, Wyoming, in July of 2009.

In addition to my office mates, Ron and Andy, I was introduced to one of my mentors and heroes in the practice of law, S. Rafe Foreman. Rafe practiced with his dear friend and fellow TLC sister, Susan Hutchison, in Flower Mound, Texas. I joked—half-joked—that these

Worth Dying For
L. Todd Kelly

two were what I hoped my partner, Heidi, and I would be like *when we grew up*. They were simply magical together.

In addition to the trial techniques that I knew I wanted to learn, I was also learning that in order to *walk in my client's hide*, I first had to know myself at a level much more profound than I had allowed up to this point, and probably better than I wanted to, at that time, given my behavior with women.

The methodology for both of these lofty goals was a process known as psychodrama—the re-enacting of events to stir emotion, memory, and creativity.

The first week of Trial Lawyers' College was dedicated to engaging in personal, inward-looking, psychodramatic work. It was work that had to be done *on the horse*. I showed up open to the process mainly due to the preparatory work that my friends had done with me. I was awakened to the fact that my trauma was coming from many aspects of my life: second-hand stress from cases I had been trying to help on, a marriage that was failing miserably, my own rejection of God's call on my life—just to name the top three demons I had to deal with. There were undoubtedly others. AJ's betrayal was not on the surface but was not very far below.

I learned to open up more with my clients and it was okay to share how their stories affected me. After all, these same stories would be told to a jury at some point, right? How these stories impact the listener is the heart of our craft. I was ready to change, and to face

Worth Dying For
L. Todd Kelly

the world with this newfound openness and honesty I had been shown.

    But when I got back home, despite doing my best to listen and hear more about Marysue's concerns about our marriage, the kids, the house, the mortgage, the high utility costs, Meghan's dates…I chose not to discuss my feelings with her. I simply told my wife I had enjoyed the class and was glad to return home. I exercised escapism and ultimately fell back into my old routines.

Worth Dying For
L. Todd Kelly

FATHER'S LOVE. A Father's Love should be honest and not feigned. Anything less is transparent.

FATHER'S LIFE. A Father's Life is about his children. While it is okay, even commanded, to love others, you should never do so at the expense of the love for the children God has blessed you with.

FATHER'S FEAR. A Father's Fear related to his family must center on the relationships with the family.

FATHER'S FIGHT. A Father's Fight is to love his children in a Godly way, while loving others well, too.

FATHER'S WISDOM. A Father's Wisdom will guide him to treat all people as God intended.

Worth Dying For
L. Todd Kelly

RIDE OR DIE

29

Falling

Riding high on my success,
I felt that I was at my best,
My confidence was on display,
And nothing I saw, caused dismay.

Especially that pretty girl,
I did not know would change my world.
Such a distant, unlikely chance,
That she and I would ever dance.

So talk to her without concern,
I didn't know that fire'd burn,
Not just inside this heart of mine,
But in hers, too, we intertwine.

Forbidden lust, this cannot go,
But she's so young and I so old.

It's just a thought, some sinful dreams,
Besides her interests, it seems,

Are focused not on me at all.
Perhaps that's why my guard did fall.
My feelings for this woman grew,
It seems she had them in her, too.

After longing for that kiss so long,
It hit just like romance in song.
My heart was taken in her hand,
My life was now like shifting sand.

To regain focus, turn away,
I'll deal with this another day.
Another needs me, I must go to work,
This duty is one I can't shirk.

•••••••••••

We were on our way to the U.S. Supreme Court in the Jones case on the landmark issue of the enforceability of mandatory, pre-dispute, confidential, binding

Worth Dying For
L. Todd Kelly

arbitration provisions. It would affect the outcome for sexual assault victims throughout our nation from this point forward. It could turn the tide of these assaults by holding corporations that permit these atrocities accountable. I was also going to argue a case at the United States Supreme Court!

Before the case was heard at the Supreme Court level, we gained considerable ground on legislation pending in Congress…enough ground in fact that the corporation withdrew the Supreme Court appeal. Though disappointed that I didn't get to argue in the highest court of our land, I was relieved that I had won that particular issue. Against all odds, we would get a trial of Jamie's case in federal district court! There were no further hurdles to clear.

We had succeeded as the pointy end of a spear, which would now bring justice to many other women waiting for this one to pierce the armor.

We've done it!

That victory alone filled me with a pride more incredible than I had ever experienced. I searched the internet for the next best story about *my victory*. I created scrapbooks of these accolades, basking in my victory's glow.

> BUT PRIDE, AS YOU KNOW, IS DANGEROUS,
> AND BLINDED BY ITS ALLURE,
> I HAD NEVER BEEN WEAKER.

Worth Dying For
L. Todd Kelly

Robbye Delle Bryan, a student at the South Texas College of Law, came to work for me when her friend, a classmate of hers who worked for me as an intern, Marissa Giovenco, told her that she'd enjoy interning at The Kelly Law Firm and that I was the type of boss who'd be understanding when she had to go home to visit with her dying grandfather who had just been diagnosed with terminal cancer. Of course, I would be understanding. What kind of plaintiff's lawyer would I be if I didn't care enough about people to understand the loss of a family member?

As I frequently do when bringing on a new employee, I checked out Robbye's social media posts on Facebook. Typical, fun-loving, law school stuff. She had family from West Texas. Like my East Texas roots, they were country to the core. I liked that. She was a red head when I met her but she has intermittently been blond, shades of brunette, and rainbow-colored since then. Her bright blue eyes—or green, depending on the light—complimented the light freckles she had, earned during her childhood summers in the sun. Her disposition was bubbly, gentle, and kind. I didn't realize at first the pain she was hiding behind her pretty smile and funny (but awkward) jokes.

Robbye was ambitious; she had her eye set on becoming a prosecutor or going into the FBI after graduation. Laudable goals, for sure. Since my career started with similar objectives, I took it on as my personal mission to educate her—to change her mind. That well-intended goal led to close talks and discussions about the practice of law as a personal injury plaintiff's trial lawyer, and to quite a bit of one-

Worth Dying For
L. Todd Kelly

on-one time I didn't mind sharing. Robbye was fun to be around and easy to look at.

As I endeavored to fill the role as her mentor, Robbye and I bonded and became close friends. Conversations about legal strategy soon turned into more intimate discussions about family and personal topics. Neither of us wanted or expected more to come from our friendship. We worked in close proximity whenever we could and appeared to be attracted to each other; it showed when she brushed by me as we passed one another.

It would be wrong, we agreed.

I would steal glimpses of her as I stood over her computer station.

It would be cliché, we agreed again.

Robbye made it clear that she did not want to be *the other woman.*

I connected to Robbye once as she and Marissa stood behind me editing a legal brief. Just as I started to type, Robbye would say aloud the phrase I was about to use. It seemed funny then, but the connection was obvious—we were entirely in tune.

Then, on another occasion, I casually brushed against her while editing a document on her computer. I felt a chill run down my spine when we touched. I would later learn that she felt it, too. There was undeniable electricity between us. The connection was just too strong to be denied. Every time I walked near her, I looked for an excuse to stop and talk to her.

Worth Dying For
L. Todd Kelly

It would be destructive, and neither of us wanted that. I had caused enough destruction. Still, although we agreed, we seemed to find excuses to touch.

We tried to ignore the feelings of mutual attraction we shared for one another. Those feelings grew anyway.

I started to work late.

So did she.

Robbye was cute. We both tried to ignore our feelings. A million reasons raced through my mind trying to convince me to leave her alone and just let it be:

I'm too old for her

I tried to convince myself; after all, a twenty-year age difference is no small gap.

I am married.

She is dating other guys.

I tried to focus on work; I walked away from her. But I could not stop thinking about her.

Things at home were not good, and when I was with Robbye, I felt wanted and respected. Respect wasn't something I'd felt at home for quite some time.

Robbye was a victim of a prior sexual assault. She was keenly aware of the emotions such a violent act evoked and provided keen insight into how to work with Jamie. She was sensitive and intuitive. I asked her to help me with the case. She was masterful—though still a law school student.

Worth Dying For
L. Todd Kelly

I wanted her. At first, I tried to tell myself that the momentary pleasure would not be worth the damage again. I tried to move past it, but still, I wanted her.

My heart was set on her, but I convinced myself that she must remain, despite my desires, just a cute intern from South Texas College of Law about which I fantasized.

I admitted these feelings to almost no one. The exception to that rule was my close friend, Ron Estefan. Ron had been my friend since the inception of the Kelly Law Firm, running his own solo practice out of the same suite and teaching me the methods of trial skills I worked on at the Trial Lawyers' College. Ron and I tried a case using the methods before I was accepted to the Trial Lawyers' College. I trusted Ron with my secret because I was somehow compelled to share it with someone, and he had long since become a confidant.

After work one evening, Robbye and I were talking, and she expressed a view of herself that was not flattering. She was having a difficult time. I had to leave the office but asked for her cell phone number. We talked for most of my hour-long drive home, and I desperately wanted to be there for her. I wanted to help her. Mostly, I wanted her to know how truly beautiful she was inside and out to me. I recall telling her, "I just wish you could see yourself through my eyes."

Working together as closely as we did, mainly when dealing with the raw and often troubling emotions from our cases, especially the Jamie Leigh Jones rape case, Robbye and I eventually came to admit that our feelings for each other had turned romantic and that we had felt the pull from very early on.

Worth Dying For
L. Todd Kelly

Nevertheless, we agreed to refrain from acting on those emotions in any physical way. That agreement seemed only to fan the flames. I was truly, madly, and deeply in love with her. It didn't take long before our agreement to keep ourselves apart hit an end.

While Robbye was celebrating a friend's birthday at dinner near the office, I called her to chat and catch up. She told me where she was, and since she was nearby, she asked if I wanted to swing by. I did. Robbye met me at my truck and jumped in. The emotion of the day, her beautiful dress, and how she looked at me. I leaned in...

We kissed. Finally! The secret between us was officially out, and the emotional tinder box was open.

The following week, we attended a settlement hearing in district court in Houston for the final resolution of a settlement on behalf of a child who had suffered a serious birth injury. The trip was purely professional and intended for her education. Despite that barrier having been shattered, I did not plan on more. On the way back to the office, however, we couldn't avoid discussing our feelings for one another. I pulled over to continue the discussion out of the earshot of our officemates.

On that long narrow stretch of road in Memorial Park on that ride home from the Harris County District Courthouse, I told her, for the first time, "I love you." Then, again, we kissed.

I never want this kiss to end.

My partner, Heidi, who had been on maternity leave when Robbye first started at the firm, returned to

Worth Dying For
L. Todd Kelly

the office a few weeks later. Her uncanny ability to read me, born of our close friendship, betrayed my *well-kept secret* about Robbye. As I walked by Heidi's office and poked my head in to say hello, she looked up at me and drummed her fingers along her desk as though to say, "You are in trouble!"

Who owns this firm, anyway?

"Everything okay?" I asked, knowing that something was wrong and not wanting her to actually answer my question.

"Really?! The intern!" She scoffed, looking at me as if I had lost my mind.

When I told Robbye about the exchange with Heidi, she immediately resigned from her position at the firm. We continued to see each other, but we decided it should not happen at the office—especially since we needed to keep our relationship discreet.

My focus promptly turned back to the one area in my life where I had clarity in my focus—the Jones case.

Kellogg, Brown & Root, one of the largest government military contractors I sued in the case, owned one of the sky-rise buildings in downtown Houston. As if by coincidence, also housed in that building was the local office of the federal Internal Revenue Service. The last clear sign that I was fighting an enemy I could not compete with came precisely 30 days before opening statements were scheduled in Jones. I had never undergone a tax audit before (and I have never been audited since)—and I do not believe in coincidence. But on that May afternoon, when the IRS tax auditors contacted me, I knew it was intended to distract me from focusing on the most important case of my career.

I called my CPA. "I cannot focus on an audit right now, Mark. I have a fiduciary duty to Jamie to put her interests ahead of mine. I need you to handle this." I tried to ignore the threat at my door.

As Jamie's trial commenced, I stood by her side, with my friend, Ron Estefan, as my co-counsel. The trial lasted for three whole weeks—an eternity in Federal Court. Press crews were waiting for us every day—like buzzards over decaying meat as we left the courthouse.

WE BELIEVED WE WERE WINNING AND KNEW OUR CAUSE WAS TRUE.

As I delivered the closing argument in the case, I became emotional. I turned to my friend, Jamie, whom I had been *protecting* for almost five years. "I can no longer protect you," I tell her before the jury. "You're in their hands, now." I then sat down, exhausted, as I released her fate to a federal jury of her peers.

I gambled it all—my reputation, my money, my firm, my future, my children's future, and my career on one case that I believed in—that I *still* believe in. Jamie's case had to be my redemption.

The jury deliberated for ten hours over two days. We were confident we had won—we could feel the stress from the defense lawyers as they paced the hallways. We had to fight to contain our excitement to project professionalism.

Worth Dying For
L. Todd Kelly

In the moments when I allowed myself to think about what the verdict would mean to me, I was sure that we had also saved my law firm. I wondered, *what settlement might they offer to avoid a large verdict?* As I imagined how the jury would punish these evil companies and send a loud message—the only way it can and then engaged in a little daydreaming:

Can I retire?

Can I pay off the house and send the wolves to another door?

Can I buy a beach house?

But, in one devastating answer, the jury crushed those dreams. My entire world seemed torpedoed with one unexpected blow that stripped Jamie of justice, ended The Kelly Law Firm, and eviscerated my personal goodwill and reputation in the press. They simply didn't believe her story.

They didn't believe in this case that I had found Worthy and been willing to die for.

Worth Dying For
L. Todd Kelly

FATHER'S LOVE. A Father's Love should focus on his family over the pressures of this world and certainly over its temptations.

FATHER'S LIFE. A Father's Life is about family, so your focus must be on family. When you lose this focus, you risk losing everything.

FATHER'S FEAR. A Father's Fear can cause him to do things that he will regret in the eyes of his children and of the Lord.

FATHER'S FIGHT. A Father's Fight is to focus on what truly matters and not be misled by the things of this world, no matter how alluring.

FATHER'S WISDOM. A Father's Wisdom will keep him from making foolish decisions when the enemy tells him, "the risk is worth it."

RETROSPECTION, REASON, AND THE REAL WORLD

30

LOSER

When you've lost in front of everyone
Your life, it seems, has come undone.
Pride, its own ferocious beast,
Took over, and it never ceased.

Winning trials and seeking fame,
Seemed all that mattered in this "game,"
Until the time came to pay up,
And none of that could fill my cup.

I hadn't been the man I should,
I hadn't really been that good.
I cheated on my wife—no shame.
Again, I thought it's just a game.

My victory would tell my story,
As I walked around in glory.

Nothing else I'd lost would show
I'd simply bask in fortune's glow.

How easily we are deceived,
Until of fortune, we're relieved.
Sitting in the stillness now,
I fell so far and don't know how.

I cannot face my family, friends
I guess this is how it ends.
In shame, disgrace, and all alone,
Unless I could somehow atone.

Perhaps there might be a way,
To lift my head again someday?
That just a dream, you stupid boozer,
Don't you see, you're just a loser.

•••••••••••

AFTER THAT VERDICT, I dissected this case many times (and I likely will for the rest of my life). As I wrestled with the details of the rulings. I imagined all sorts of untoward happenings behind the scenes.

Worth Dying For
L. Todd Kelly

Of course, something else had happened—they sent the IRS into my office, right?

I put everything I had into that case, and I had put it above everything else: my time, my money, my emotions, my reputation, my credibility, my children, my faith...everything. I believed I had to truly *put my money where my mouth is*—yet I'd lost.

I FELT FROZEN IN TIME, UNABLE TO MOVE, TO THINK, TO UNDERSTAND ANYTHING OTHER THAN THE REALITY THAT I'D LOST EVERYTHING.

More importantly, I'd lost the battle for this courageous woman I had grown to love: Jamie Jones.

I found myself tormented; I took on the responsibility to protect her, and to achieve justice for her—yet in the end, I had failed her.

I was crushed and offended each time Jamie's integrity was challenged in the press—but I was now powerless to respond. I needed to protect her *against all enemies*, regardless of where they came from. I had dedicated years to protecting her—and in the end, I failed her.

Worth Dying For
L. Todd Kelly

I suddenly feel powerless to help her. I am crushed under the weight of this loss and the simultaneous collapse of my personal life. Was I always inadequate? Probably. And, I have:

FAILED my family—repeatedly.
FAILED Robbye.
FAILED my law firm.
FAILED my partner, Heidi.
FAILED my brother, Reagan.
FAILED my friend and trial partner, Ron.

I didn't wear that failure publicly. I wouldn't. I somehow *still* remained too proud. I wallowed in my own self-destruction, however. As I look back, I see this was Satan's playground: a defeated man who had become separated from and lost his way back to the Savior. Like the following rendition of a "Reverse Psalm 23."

FOREVER

I appeared to have lost everything:
I've left the Lord, my shepherd. I am wanting.
I am unable to lie down in green pastures.
I find myself in chaotic waters.
My soul is exhausted.
I walk down paths in the wrong direction.
As I walk through the valley of the shadow of death,
I fear every evil, for God is not with me.
There is no rod nor staff to comfort me.
I go hungry before my enemies.
I have lost the anointing and am desperate for blessing.
Goodness and mercy do not follow me, but I
must chase them every day of my life.
I will not dwell in the house of the Lord forever.

~ Pastor Avery and Zion Montgomery

Worth Dying For
L. Todd Kelly

After three days of staring aimlessly at an idiot box in front of the leather recliner in my bedroom, into which I had sunken deeply, I pry myself out of that leather tomb and crawl to the closet to find my cold, black Beretta.

Well cared for—like any good Marine's weapon.

As I pick it up. I almost caress the cold, metal barrel, the rough hand grips.

I smell the CLR cleaning fluid on the metal. I feel the slightly oily surface of its protection from rust.

I pull the slide back with my left hand to lock it in place.

As I release the catch with my right thumb, the slide chambers a hollow-point round with an almost echo. The familiar noise is ominous this time.

I flip the safety upwards with my thumb, exposing the red dot below the safety catch.

LOCKED AND LOADED.

Slowly, I lift the instrument of destruction to my mouth. Tears well in my eyes as I realize this loss is worth dying for. There is no rush—no one is home. I am utterly alone.

MY MULTIPLE FAILURES ARE WORTH DYING FOR.

Worth Dying For
L. Todd Kelly

FATHER'S LOVE. A Father's Love needs to remain focused on his family rather than on the things he desires for himself.

FATHER'S LIFE. A Father's Life can unravel without focusing on God and his family.

FATHER'S FEAR. A Father's Fear can lead him to severe shame if he fails to keep his eye on God.

FATHER'S FIGHT. A Father's Fight is to avoid failing those he loves and respects.

FATHER'S WISDOM. A Father's Wisdom will keep him from destroying those in his path and, ultimately, himself.

WHEN LIFE ROCKS YOU TO THE CORE

31

THE WARRIOR

The trust she placed in me: complete.
Her life she'd laid down at my feet,
My confidence was more than strong,
I had waited for this case for so long.

Then came the time to show the world
That I was the one to help this girl.
But victories had made me weak
I did not know I'd reached my peak.

We made it public—for all to see.
Pride snuck in—it now owned me.
I'll win this case and in the press.
The world will see my very best.

The world will see a hero, right?
Perhaps there should have been some fright...
The jury fought ten hours plus.
Certainly, they'd ruled for us?

But they answered the first question, "No."

A feeling from deep inside did grow.
It stung a bit but wasn't done.
Before it left, I was the one...

The one who sat alone at home
Thoughts of worthlessness did roam.
Others would not share this strife.
For a while I thought I'd end my life.

What could pull me through this grief?
What could bring me some relief?
That Beretta sat just feet away.
But pain was not all that I'd slay.

Others cared—and I knew it too.
But I didn't want them close, that's true.
Shame had taken o'er my heart.
Then I looked back at the start.

I believed I'd built this story.
That I deserved the fame, the glory.

Worth Dying For
L. Todd Kelly

Arrogance, conceit, and pride.
Were all that I now held inside.

Let it go, I'm just one part
Of a larger tale that is the art.
The art of life, and love, and loss,
That like a ship on waves will toss.

I cannot stop the rolling seas,
Or this self-inflicted pain appease.
So take this pride and foolish shame,
I'm only strong when I am lame.

Now remember who you truly are
Stop trying to be someone's star.
Just love your friends, your kids, your wife
The rest is just your busy strife.

The job you do, it matters, sure.
But it's not you, so do not pour
Your whole life into the voice of twelve,
For if you do, your soul you shelve.

Keep your focus on what counts
Know that when the battle mounts
You'll do your best to make it right.
But sometimes evil wins the fight.

Live to fight another day
Do not throw all you've been away.
Put down the gun, lift up your head.
And choose to go back in—instead.

A warrior does not win each fight
But continues on with all his might.
A warrior would not walk away
This warrior will not die today

•••••●●●●●•••

I HAD NEITHER showered nor shaved since the jury returned its verdict in favor of these military contractors, depriving my dear friend, Jamie, of justice.

Worth Dying For
L. Todd Kelly

I smelled of body odor and Scotch. My hair was matted—but short. I was disgusting, even to myself.

I wasn't even sure if I had even eaten. If I had, it was only because of the kindness of a woman I once loved; a wife, who had born me three children with whom I usually could not get along. She had been more supportive through this loss than I deserved.

I sat before a television that merely provided background clatter, protecting me from the haunting silence. I had not watched a single show—except the occasional news story about my humiliating defeat. I stayed glued to those stories…hoping and dreaming that the punchline might be different next time.

I had considered quitting the law on several occasions in the past. I could teach Karate full-time. I found great joy in teaching those kids about self-defense. But, I could not afford my kids' college on sensei's pay. What pay? I barely paid the overhead at the dojo with the tuition from karate students.

I would have to sell the house. I had built it *to die in*. It now appeared that wouldn't happen. The irony of that phrase was not lost on me.

I wondered if I could start a lawn care company. That would have been far less emotionally taxing. I recalled my business evaluation of a koi pond construction company. *I'm still young enough*, I thought.

My in-laws had moved out into a retirement community. This was too much house, anyway

Worth Dying For
L. Todd Kelly

I WAS SUPPOSED TO BE ONE OF THE GOOD GUYS!

Wait, I was hated before. Perhaps I deserved this?

I should have stayed in the Corps to defend my name when AJ betrayed me. At least there, I knew where my next meal was coming from, and I never lacked for a job to do. It wasn't easy, but this wasn't either. In the Corps, I could gain confidence in my physical ability, if nothing else. Here, I was bathing in my failures, alone.

How did I put myself in this mess? *Chasing justice?* Why had I not learned that justice is just an illusion?

HOW COULD I HAVE FOUND THIS TO BE WORTH DYING FOR?

Worth Dying For
L. Todd Kelly

FATHER'S LOVE. A Father's Love must not only be present internally but must also be displayed to his children.

FATHER'S LIFE. A Father's Life is valuable to his family, even when he no longer sees the value himself.

FATHER'S FEAR. A Father's Fear of shame can lead him directly to what he is ashamed of. Only God can relieve a man's shame.

FATHER'S FIGHT. A Father's Fight is to avoid focusing on the world and to remain focused on God.

FATHER'S WISDOM. A Father's Wisdom will not suffice unless the wisdom comes from the Ultimate Father in Heaven.

BUT GOD

3 2

THE PRICE

He didn't leave me, as I deserve,
But as I tried to calm my nerves,
He showed me exactly what I needed,
Though His love I had not heeded.

My Father was there with me that day,
The price, He didn't make me pay.

Instead, he bore that weight alone.
When for my sin, he did atone.

I do not want my kids to see,
The things that I did — just for me.
But thankfully, my Father saved,
Despite the way that I've behaved.

•••••••••••

THOUGH THIS IS where it started, this is also where this book would have ended, except that God was there with me. He was in that closet right by my side—as He had always been on every part of my journey.

My Father knew my heart. He never left me, even though I had refused to see Him.

It is He who showed me, in vivid detail, what my children would have found on the floor of that closet if I had finished what Satan had enticed me to do. Leaving my kids with that final image of their father—on the floor, bleeding from the back of what would be left of my head, and holding the instrument of my self-inflicted death was more than I could do to them—and God knew it.

Worth Dying For
L. Todd Kelly

While I didn't feel Him that day, He was there. He was holding me, and He was loving me. All while I was too blind to reach for Him.

I imagined their pain. I feared their last memory of me somehow giving them permission to follow in that path when things get too tough in their own lives. They don't have that permission. I would not (and will not) give it to them.

In the end, I could not leave this world that way.

I put the Beretta back in its bag.

Sadly, many of my colleagues have made a different choice. Many of my brother and sister trial lawyers who take on the *secondary stress* of those for whom we fight every single day could not find a way out of their own closets. Equally sad is the reality that many of my colleagues did not rebound from the stress imposed upon them by the career they chose. As they held the triggers of their own pistols to their heads, there was no one there to tell them, "Don't do it!" or convince them not to pull. They ignored the messages that God sent them. Many others ignored Him completely.

I write this book as a plea to not pull the trigger!

OUR CAREERS, AND EVEN OUR CLIENTS, ARE SIMPLY NOT WORTH DYING FOR.

Worth Dying For
L. Todd Kelly

FATHER'S LOVE. The Father's Love is about forgiveness and understanding, even when His children do not obey.

FATHER'S LIFE. The Father's Life is given to his children, regardless of the children's behavior.

FATHER'S FEAR. The Father's Fear is that his children will turn from Him and not return.

FATHER'S FIGHT. The Father's Fight is for the souls of His children, whom He loves.

FATHER'S WISDOM. THE Father's Wisdom is perfect knowledge of what to show His children and when.

THEY NEED YOU

33

Needed

I'm no longer prepared to fight.
I've stared at walls all through the night.
But she was beaten worse than me,
And back to fight, her simple plea.

I didn't think that I could go,
But courage is now on show.

As I went back to help the others,
Sisters, daughters, and their mothers.

I find my strength in her simple plea:
This task was never about me.
These women need my help I know,
So showered and shaved, to work I go

••••••••••••

As I crawled out of my closet and returned to the recliner where I had spent the last three days, I was deflated, exhausted, and overcome with grief.

As I sat there waiting for something to happen, my cell phone rang.

"What are you doing, Todd?" It was Jamie.

"Nothing, Jamie. Just sitting here."

"I hear you haven't gone back to work yet?"

"No."

"Don't you think you should?" she asked.

"I don't know if I can," I admitted, defeated.

"You have at least three other women victimized by the same company. Those are just the ones I know of…" Then came her magic words: "…They need you."

Worth Dying For
L. Todd Kelly

At those three words, I got up. I washed my face. I shaved. I went back to the office.

I knew she was right—they did need me. These women needed me to protect them in the same manner that I tried to protect Jamie. I knew that they had no chance without someone fighting for them. At that moment, I was all they had.

They needed me to ignore the naysayers in the press who would denigrate Jamie and her attorney.

They needed me to spend more borrowed money and they needed to eat up more of my time. They needed me to stand face-to-face with the most significant military contractor in the world as if I could outspend them: to stare them down with confidence while I stood there shrouded in my own terror.

They needed me to be what I didn't know if I still had the strength or courage to continue to be—a trial lawyer.

Somehow, I stood. Somehow, I fulfilled my role. Somehow, I helped.

Several victims were ultimately compensated for the devastation to their bodies and the indignities they suffered overseas. I cannot say more than this because of the confidentiality provisions in their agreements, but I am proud of the work my team did for THEM.

It turns out I also needed them.

They thanked me and moved on. Their lives would be better now.

So would mine.

But The Kelly Law Firm, P.C., had taken its final, fatal blow. That firm died in the pursuit of justice.

Worth Dying For
L. Todd Kelly

FATHER'S LOVE. The Father's Love comes from places that we often do not suspect.

FATHER'S LIFE. The Father's Life is an example of service to others, even when He did not want to sacrifice.

FATHER'S FEAR. The Father's Fear is only that His children do not follow him.

FATHER'S FIGHT. The Father's Fight is for His children

FATHER'S WISDOM. The Father's Wisdom is revealed in His way to those who seek Him and listen to His reply.

Worth Dying For
L. Todd Kelly

LEADERS EAT LAST

34

BY MY OWN HAND

The end is near, at last, it seems.
I've turned to nightmares, what were once dreams.
But the spark that keeps me up at night,
Has started to appear so bright.

The work we did to then discover,
That she was more than just a lover.
I do not know how life could be,
If her loving face I could not see.

But harm I'm going to do, I know,
But this path is one on which I'll go.
The hurt that I am bound to cause
Is not one I can keep on pause.

As I move forward toward my fate,
I hope my children will not hate.

The pain is great and it is shared
With those for whom I have most cared.

My business, too, will hurt some others,
Friends to me, fathers, mothers.
I hate that I have let them down
After we enjoyed such great renown.

Behind in pay, I have just my word.
Is that enough, for they have heard
That I would pay them when I can.
How much longer will they trust this man?

I pay them with what funds come in,
What a far cry from where I'd been.
They're paid with remnants from my past,
With nothing left, I am paid last.

• • • • • • • • • • •

Worth Dying For
L. Todd Kelly

BEFORE I CLOSED THE doors to my firm for the last time, I returned to "The Ranch" for a graduate course. I had already paid for it, at any rate.

By the time I trek back to attend that graduate course of the Trial Lawyers' College at Thunderhead Ranch in Dubois, Wyoming, I knew and had admitted to myself and Robbye, that I was hopelessly in love with her. We had now been *outed*, as our feelings for one another had grown too strong to conceal from anyone nearby. We tried not to go out publicly because I was still married, but it was clear that Robbye had my heart. I was miserable in my marriage at that point, but in knowing *right from wrong*, I struggled.

I was chosen as the protagonist in a psychodrama about this raging internal conflict in the "Johnson Barn" at the ranch, directed by Don Clarkson, a master at the craft. Don Clarkson may well be one of the most talented psycho-dramatists alive.

Don directed me to dig inward and face the choice that I would inevitably have to make. As he directed, I chose people in the room to play the roles of Robbye, Marysue, and each of my children.

Don chose Joey Low, a fellow Marine, to play my conscience. With Joey yelling in my ear about doing the right thing and the faces of my wife and children looking at me, I had difficulty looking at Robbye (played by my now dear friend, Lori Gingery).

I initially made the *right choice* to stay with Marysue, but I was literally in tears on the barn floor because I could not accept losing Robbye. Don directed…"The wonderful thing about psychodrama is that we get to

Worth Dying For
L. Todd Kelly

make every choice—to see what works—so get up and choose again!"

I got up and made the other choice. Holding tightly to my friend, Lori Gingery, in her auxiliary role as Robbye, I felt the pain of loss, but nothing like I had just felt when I chose to live without her. I knew the loss of Marysue would hurt, as would the loss of respect from my kids that I knew would likely follow. I feared that my children would turn from me, and didn't know how long they would remain that way—or if they would ever accept me back into their lives.

After the psychodramatic re-enactment and the work of that session, I knew there was no painless way out of my situation. I was going to hurt someone, actually several people, and I was going to hurt, too. That much was inevitable. But, there was one choice: I simply could not live if I let Robbye go, of that I was sure. Now, I knew what I must do – as hard as it would be.

After the psychodrama exercise, I jokingly told Don many times that he was responsible for my life.

"I don't want that responsibility!" was always Don's reply.

My response remains forever in my heart. "Don, you have my gratitude for guiding me to the most significant, life-giving decision I have ever made."

I watched this man, and other psychodramatists at the Trial Lawyers College change many lives. I've seen them help countless trial lawyers deal with the demons and pain borne out of this industry. But this time it was me. It was deeply personal, and it was transformative.

Worth Dying For
L. Todd Kelly

That day, his skills helped me to make a decision I could not have made on my own.

I do not advocate divorce for anyone, but I now know that I am forgiven for that choice, and for the choices I made that led up to that point.

The personal drama surrounding my break-up with Marysue once I returned from the ranch, is omitted here to preserve the privacy surrounding the issues between her, myself, and my adult kids. Suffice it to say that it was extremely painful—for all of us. I had betrayed my children, and I had betrayed the vows I made to their mother. I felt worthless as a husband, as a father, as a man, as a human.

Heidi, whose children still referred to me as *Uncle Todd*, closed the door to my office and turned to speak. Before she could utter a word, I saw a tear form in her right eye and roll down her right cheek. Heidi, who was usually unemotional and guarded could not speak; her chin quivered.

I had never seen Heidi this way. I got up from behind my desk and met her halfway. I hugged her and let her cry. Her sentiment was kind, but the words she could not form had already hurt me to my core.

"You don't have to say it, Heidi, I understand. Do you have a place to land?"

"Yes," she sobbed.

Heidi had not been paid in several months. She had been holding on, hoping—like me—for a breakthrough that never came. And she was loyal. She had continued to hope that we might pull out a miracle in the end.

"I owe you some money," I said to her. "I have one last settlement check expected, and you will be paid from that."

"I know you will do what you can."

Heidi and the others who held on were eventually paid in full.

The lawyers and staff that worked at the Kelly Law Firm, P.C. when I made the decision to permanently close the doors were mothers, fathers, husbands, wives, and, most importantly to me, they were my friends. This public closing of The Kelly Law Firm would happen simultaneously with my very public divorce.

The partner is paid last—if at all. That is the true hallmark of the *greedy trial lawyer* you hear so much bad press about. That last check was disbursed to others; not one penny of it came home.

BUT THAT PRINCIPLE WAS WORTH DYING FOR —AT LEAST FINANCIALLY TO ME.

Worth Dying For
L. Todd Kelly

FATHER'S LOVE. A Father's Love when betrayed by the father, can cause pain to everyone involved.

FATHER'S LIFE. A Father's Life, when not lived for his family, causes pain to the family and personal devastation to the man.

FATHER'S FEAR. A Father's Fear is often that his sins become public and that he is no longer respected.

FATHER'S FIGHT. A Father's Fight is to do well in the eyes of his children.

FATHER'S WISDOM. A Father's Wisdom is depended upon by a family, and when he fails them, the betrayal is profound and long-lasting.

Worth Dying For
L. Todd Kelly

THE REALITY OF SUCCESS

35

The "King" Has Fallen

Broken by my own design,
A fate that was uniquely mine.
I loved a woman I should not.
In my lies, I had been caught.

Desperate just to start again,
But how far down to just begin?
The "gold digger" with whom I now shared my life,
Was providing sustenance through her strife.

Another chance was set in sight,
The pay was low, but still, I might
Be able yet to pay my bills
And perhaps recover from my ills.

No more "the king," I take my role,
It seems my sin's taken its toll.
But this will just increase my strife,
It could have cost me my whole life.

••••••••••••

I was completely broke. And I was utterly broken. My marriage was over; I could not stay in my home.

My firm is destroyed. I have no job.

Somehow, Robbye still chose to be there for me. She remained forever my rock. Despite rumors and innuendos that inevitably follow a relationship that starts in adultery—and there were plenty—she remained my best friend and strength. Funny that some saw her as a *gold-digger*, simply because of our twenty-year age difference and a perceived wealth that was far from the reality of my situation.

Worth Dying For
L. Todd Kelly

Like my partner and the other employees who once called me *boss*, I searched for work. But who wanted to hire the man who had just so famously lost the most significant case of his life on national television—then crashed a law firm—and a family, and who did it all so publicly?

Robbye worked as a legal brief drafter with another plaintiff's office, The Mostyn Law Firm. She had accepted that position when she passed the bar exam. It was not possible to return to the Kelly Law Firm since our feelings for one another had become known to Heidi, and we could not conceal our affection.

Robbye's paycheck paid the rent several times because I did not have the money. I could no longer live in the house I had built *to die in*, as my soon-to-be ex-wife and my children needed and deserved that home. Eventually, it would be sold, and the proceeds divided in the divorce.

I didn't want to practice law anymore. It had beaten me. But I had no other transferrable skills at my age that could dent the student loan debt that Robbye and I were both strapped with. My kids didn't seem to understand why Daddy couldn't pay for their student loans (I had always thought I would and told them so).

The prominent place to turn in this situation was to God, but I was too ashamed to even do that! I was fervent that I would not do so—despite the trouble it had created for me, I had not yet dropped my foolish pride, even though I knew because it was too big for me—I needed to give this situation to Him. I simply could not get out of my own way.

Worth Dying For
L. Todd Kelly

Eventually, Bruce Phillips, a friend and fellow lawyer from the Trial Lawyers' College, whom I met through Ron, returned my call. Bruce worked in the San Antonio office of The Carlson Law Firm, a prominent plaintiff's firm in Central Texas. I remembered how much he raved about the firm he worked for and knew it was a more prominent firm that might have a spot for me.

He arranged an interview with the firm's owner, Craig Carlson, in Killeen, Texas. Craig, it turned out, is a man of God. Where I relied upon my own talents to run a law firm (and we all saw where that led), Craig had relied upon his faith in God to lead him to make relationships and to deal as his faith commands.

The difference in results was stark: he ran one of the state's largest, most successful firms, if not the country. I, on the other hand, ran my firm to crash and burn in a public, humiliating death. It would take me a while to attribute the different outcomes to the One responsible.

CRAIG HAD UNDERSTOOD WHAT WAS WORTH DYING FOR.

Like the prodigal I am, I was still too lost to see it. I had not lived in the devastation I created quite long enough…

Worth Dying For
L. Todd Kelly

FATHER'S LOVE. The Father's Love is there for all—even when we do not see it or even when we run from it.

FATHER'S LIFE. The Father's Life is full of love and redemption for those who will accept it.

FATHER'S FEAR. The Father's Fear is only for his children to fail to accept him, condemning them to separation from Him.

FATHER'S FIGHT. The Father's Fight is with the will of men who choose the world's ways rather than His ways.

FATHER'S WISDOM. The Father's Wisdom is complete, and those who trust in Him have the advantage of an all-knowing Father.

Worth Dying For
L. Todd Kelly

THE PHOENIX ALWAYS RISES

36

Rise

Lady Justice winks. She winks a lot.
I listened and absorbed this thought.
We speak of justice—hard fought for
At home and far off of our shore.

The document that guides our art,
Drafted that we not drift apart.
Yet, as applied, she isn't blind,
Results are not always so kind.

Peeking out from beneath her shield
As she oversees the field,
She guides the way she thinks she should,
Sometimes that Lady can't see the good.

To protect our treasured way of life,
And honor the sacrifice and strife,
I use the ink within my skin
To remind me I must rise again.
If we're to live as was the dream,
We must be more than what we seem
To raise the causes with which we're charged
Our vision must be now enlarged.

We rise again to fight once more,
That's why we get up off the floor.
For if we fail to rise again,
The Lady will not save good men.

We rise not just because we should,
We rise because we do some good.
We have to struggle and to fight,
Sometimes with every ounce of might.

Lest we hear our client's cries,
Let's return the blinder o'er her eyes
So when the lady tries to wink,
It's only justice that we think

Should be applied in this, our cause.
For if it's otherwise, let's pause:
"We lost our way along this path,"
Will be this nation's epitaph.

••••••••••••

THE POSITION THAT CRAIG Carlson offered me in Austin was a severe blow to my once hyper-inflated ego. I had been a partner in two firms with my name on the door. I had recently owned one of them. I still owned it. It was just not open or viable. I was to start over as an associate.

Then there was the issue of pay—at less than half of my base pay when I was running my own firm (in the months when I was paid) and less than I had been paid by other firms even ten years earlier. I seemed natural to initially be insulted at the pay cut to well beneath what I was worth even ten years earlier—but simultaneously, I was desperate to take it, as I had not seen an actual paycheck in months and had been surviving off of Robbye's generosity. I had no choice but to accept. It was August 2012.

Despite the blow to my ego and self-perceived status, the position and the pay were welcome changes—from running a failing firm and not being paid—to living on what money Robbye could bring home.

After nearly eleven years as a Marine Officer, I was adorned with not one bit of body ink. There was one close call while out on liberty as a young Lieutenant in Korea after consuming far too much OB Beer—but Staff Sergeant Grimes, my Staff NCO, kindly carried my limp, drunken body from the tattoo parlor and poured me into a cab to return to base camp. I was always thankful that in my drunken state I didn't get that *artist's rendition* of the Eagle, Globe & Anchor emblazoned on my left arm—or wherever else.

Worth Dying For
L. Todd Kelly

Robbye had several small tattoos, and I had considered getting one, too. I was by myself in Austin, Texas, following a successful job interview with Craig Carlson, and didn't want to drive back to Houston alone. Robbye was away on a girl's weekend trip anyway, so it was just an empty rental waiting there.

I found *Diablo Rojo*. A little tattoo studio across from the University of Texas Campus. And on that August day in 2012 when Craig offered me the job. I decided this was as good a time as any to get tattooed.

My first experience with ink was that the pain, while accurate, is somewhat symbolic in and of itself. It hurt to plummet to where I was. This symbol should hurt. One of the clients I had helped after Jamie's loss bore a dragon tattoo across her entire back. She once told me that the tattoo symbolized the brutality with which she was brutally raped and that the pain of imprinting the ink on her was therapeutic for her. I finally understood.

The phoenix that now adorns my right shoulder was permanently etched into my skin during a three-and-a-half-hour sitting. It was (and is) a symbol and reminder of my own emergence from devastation.

I responded to Robbye's call during a break in the etching by sending her a cell phone picture of the tattoo in progress. She had been worried that I had not called her yet to report on the interview because it was getting late. I wasn't sure if she was happy or disappointed when I showed her what I was doing. She had expected me to be on the drive back to Houston rather than staying in Austin and getting my first ink.

Worth Dying For
L. Todd Kelly

Perhaps this was selfish, but I felt that I needed to do this alone. The tattoo symbolized the re-emergence—not only of me as a professional—but also as a man.

More importantly, and though I admittedly did not intend it at the time, it would later come to symbolize my re-birth as a Christian and as a forgiven son of God.

It would remind me of what was truly worth dying for.

Worth Dying For
L. Todd Kelly

FATHER'S LOVE. A Father's Love for his children is often what can urge him on.

FATHER'S LIFE. A Father's Life is not over as long as he is willing to be redeemed and repent to make that happen.

FATHER'S FEAR. A Father's Fear can keep him from God.

FATHER'S FIGHT. A Father's Fight to return to God is an example his children should follow when confronted with their sins.

FATHER'S WISDOM. A Father's Wisdom is often gained after turning from the sin that separated him from God.

THE FEAR OF REPEATING DEFEAT

37

Fresh Start

Returning to a former home,
I'm never again to roam.
I want to stop ever repeating
I want to stop my life of cheating.
I am not known in this "home" town,
Perhaps I don't want that renown.

The failures of my past are gone,
Now in this town, I can move on.

I'm welcome here and cared for, too.
I'm hoping that this life is new.
Those that do not know this life
Will never understand this strife.

•••••••••••

I STRUGGLED, AT FIRST, to regain my identity, to regain my self-respect and my dignity. Although I graduated from the University of Texas, I was new to Austin as an attorney and mainly unknown to the local bar associations. Robbye came with me; she could work remotely for her employer in Houston, the Mostyn Law Firm, and she helped pay the bills I couldn't pay.

As a benefit of my employment, Craig paid my dues to join the Capital Area Trial Lawyers' Association and renewed my lapsing membership in the Texas Trial Lawyers Association – I simply could not afford those dues on my own. Craig also paid my way back into the American Association for Justice.

For the first time in my professional history, I was timid from defeat. I still approached all new acquaintances as if they were judging me. Why wouldn't they be judging? I judged myself.

Worth Dying For
L. Todd Kelly

THE CRASH OF MY LAW FIRM WAS STILL AN OPEN WOUND IN MY VERY BEING.

The place where I had best been able to discuss it was at the Ranch. Those classmates, fellow warriors for justice, provided me with the safety to discuss my failures without judgment. They salved the wound. When my Trial Lawyers' College classmate and close friend – no, brother, Scott Webre, called to check on me and inquired about how I was doing (knowing the intense pain of losing my firm and all that experience entails), my answer set me on a path of appreciation that would take some time to fully realize and appreciate.

"I'm pretty good, Scott. I have been paid three times in the last couple of months and haven't settled a single case yet."

That is the summation of the risks we take as trial lawyers when not working as salaried associates. I was thrilled to have been paid just for going to work. That concept had been lost on me as a firm owner who was only paid after everyone else when the case was resolved.

Yes, there are some lawyers who succeed this way – some who make a lot of money. I tried to be that lawyer, and I will try again. But the unsung heroes are the many more who struggle to make ends meet and pay off the student loans they took out, believing that it would all be okay because justice is fair —those who work for justice even when it eludes them and leaves them broken and broken.

> **THESE ARE SOME OF MY HEROES. THESE PEOPLE BELIEVE THAT A CAUSE BIGGER THAN THEMSELVES IS WORTH DYING FOR.**

Worth Dying For
Todd Kell

FATHER'S LOVE. A Father's Love is sometimes lonely but should be focused on his children.

FATHER'S LIFE. A Father's Life is not always easy, and he should strive to set an example even in difficult times.

FATHER'S FEAR. A Father's Fear is often of judgment.

FATHER'S FIGHT. A Father's Fight is to strive to be better, even when the enemy reminds him of his sin.

FATHER'S WISDOM. A Father's Wisdom cannot come forward until the Father turns from worldly ways toward God.

Worth Dying For
Todd Kell

DIE TO SELF
LIVE FOR GOD

38

I'M SORRY

"Rest your soul," my Savior cries,
"Just trust yourself"—Satan lies.
The world believes the Devil's tongue
I turn from what I knew when young.

This name I've built with my hard work.
So Jesus is the man I shirk.
I walk my way and ignore His.
I've made my name, I've honed this biz.

Jesus didn't get me here,
So pass the wine, the booze, the beer.
I got up here on my own accord.
There's no obstacle I can't fjord.

The fall is hard when you fall alone.
He would have caught me if I'd atone.
I didn't ask. My pride was strong.
I had ignored Him for so long

At the bottom, when I then surveyed,
I realized the price I'd paid.
It wasn't property or fame or might,
That held the strongest, toughest bite.

It was that I turned upon the One
Who, for my sake, was so undone.
He bore my pain so great,
And I returned with worse than hate.

I ignored my Savior's pleas
So now I come upon my knees,
Forgiveness, grace is all I seek.
I've finally learned that strength is meek.

I come to You with peace and love,
That I know comes from You, above.
My arms stretched high; please hold me, God
It's me, your son, it's just me…Todd.

• • • • • • • • • • •

Worth Dying For
L. Todd Kelly

AFTER WORKING FOR A firm led by faith for a few years, Robbye entered the doors of Celebration Church in Georgetown, Texas, while I was in Houston at a trial in November of 2015. She loved the message from the pastor and called me that day to tell me that we had to go back. It was a couple of weeks before I heard Pastor Joe Champion preach. It took a couple of years before I felt like I was one of God's children again. But eventually, through prayer, obedience, and grace, that phoenix started to mean something new: It is no longer about me.

IT IS ABOUT THE ONE WHO PROVED THAT HE FOUND ME WORTH DYING FOR

Grace, that only Jesus can offer, has always been there —I just needed to get out of my own way. This is my most important message for my brothers and sisters who may be reading this. We often become so self-important with our legal (or business) acumen and our plaques on the wall that we forget that it is all a gift from our Father and that we are nothing without Him and without His grace. Alternatively, we become so entrenched in our secondary stress that we forget to rely on Him to carry us through it.

The realization that God is in charge eventually enabled me to stand again: to fight for those less fortunate and those harmed by the acts of others.

Unfortunately, when I left Virginia in 2001, I drifted away from my faith and never really found my

Worth Dying For
L. Todd Kelly

way back into church until the end of 2015, three years after joining The Carlson Law Firm.

During that interim, I enjoyed sporadic professional success and notoriety —all of which I attributed to my "heroic" efforts. That prideful arrogance set me up for the humiliating fall that, while destroying my law firm, probably saved my soul.

> PRIDE, ARROGANCE, AND ADULTERY ALSO HURT THE RELATIONSHIP THAT I HAD HOPED MY CHILDREN WOULD HAVE WITH GOD, AS THEY NOW SAW THEIR VERY HUMAN FATHER AS A HYPOCRITE.

I had failed as their father and as a servant of God in leading them to Him. I had been unfaithful to their mother—my then-wife, and to my God. More to my shame now, I had not even tried to be faithful to her. I was simply lost and on a path of self-destruction and spiritual death. I didn't care.

It was Robbye's excited phone call in 2015 telling me about hearing the message from a charismatic pastor at Celebration Church in Georgetown, Texas, that brought me back into the Body of Christ.

I was in Houston that weekend, preparing for a trial set to start on Monday. My mind was not on spiritual things. But God worked for me through Robbye.

One of the principal people God employed in my personal salvation story is Pastor Joe Champion.

Worth Dying For
L. Todd Kelly

"Pastor Joe" is about a year older than I am but infinitely wiser. Along with his wife, Lori, who is co-pastor at Celebration Church in Georgetown, Texas, this man has led an army of Christ-followers to bring hope and salvation to many, including me. His ability to apply Biblical understanding to any situation he faces has been a catalyst that grew Celebration Church from just his family of five in 2000 to over 21,000 members today.

Following God's call on his life, Pastors Joe and Lori followed the command "It is Austin," whispered simultaneously in their souls while they were physically apart but serving the Lord. In response, they obediently uprooted their young family from their comfortable home in Baton Rouge, Louisiana, to found Celebration Church. This story is miraculous and worthy of more lines than I have given it. It is a story that has shaped my own and placed me in a position to tell it. But, Celebration's is not my story to tell– at least not on these pages.

That call from Robbye and my return to the family of God saved my soul. Through Pastor Joe's teaching, God changed my life and destination. Pastor Joe's leadership guided me into salvation and a deeper walk with Christ than I have ever experienced.

Today, I am a graduate of Celebration Leadership Institute with a ministry diploma. I am again learning to walk—one step at a time.

Worth Dying For
L. Todd Kelly

Don't get me wrong. It wasn't that I didn't know Christ before I heard Pastor Joe's teaching. It was much worse than that: I knew Him, but I turned my back on Him.

Though I am ashamed of my own actions, I hope that when you read this, you will understand that God's grace alone is what saves. He saved me from the eternal fate I earned. If He will save me after I turned my back on Him, He will save you, too. Just ask.

And I know today that He was there, in that closet, filling me with the images and words that I needed to stop me from pulling that trigger.

And Jesus died an excruciating death so that neither I nor you have to.

I NOW UNDERSTAND THAT TO JESUS, I, LIKE YOU, WAS WORTH DYING FOR.

Worth Dying For
L. Todd Kelly

FATHER'S LOVE. The Father's Love is a constant that we often turn from when we forget that He is the way.

FATHER'S LIFE. The Father's Life is the example that sets men free, and all fathers should learn from Him.

FATHER'S FEAR. A Father's Fear is that he fails to set an example for his children, but that fear is resolved when a father turns to his Heavenly Father.

FATHER'S FIGHT. A Father's Fight is to turn from worldly desires, repent, and return to God.

FATHER'S WISDOM. The Father's Wisdom is unfailing and unchanging. This wisdom guides us through the trappings of this world and can be found in His Word.

Worth Dying For
L. Todd Kelly

GOD ALWAYS WINS

39

From Harm to Hallelujah

The world took it all,
But I am thankful for the fall.
When I could not see how to pay
I heard His Word and did obey.

All a sudden, my life was changed,
The math, it seemed, was so deranged.
I trusted God, He didn't fail.
My finances He did not derail.

That step in faith changed my whole life
And gave me peace from all that strife.

One step in faith was all it took,
Now, I spend time in His Book.

As I grew near, God fixed some things,
And of his glory, my heart sings.
My children, too, have seen his love
Though they've not seen it from above.

Thank you, God, for being there
And showing where to spend my care.
My busy strife is not the bother,
My life is yours. I thank you, Father.

• • • • • • • • • • • •

THINGS CHANGED WHILE WORKING for Craig. It didn't happen instantly, but change came. People started to call me again. I had some success with a few cases. Colleagues knew me from my profoundly public defeat.

"You put your money where your mouth is, didn't you?" became an all-too-common compliment.

Yeah— but I lost it all.

Worth Dying For
L. Todd Kelly

There were always knowing laughs. Not exactly funny. But it is better now.

I don't worry about money anymore. Not because I am rich or even set up for life, financially: I'm neither of those things —far from it. Perhaps one day?

For now, Robbye and I are still paying off her exorbitant student loans as well as those I took out for my children to go to college, and we are raising our beautiful daughter, Selby Jewel (named for her great-grandmothers on both sides).

I don't worry about money because I have simply learned that worrying will not make it better. I don't worry because God has told me not to: He's got this. He has proven that He is there. We began tithing, as commanded, when we didn't know how to make ends meet. Mathematically, they never could. Yet, they do. I discussed it with Pastor Joe after breakfast.

"It's God's math," he tells me.

He's right. I quit trying to make sense of it and simply accepted the gift. He is good.

I now focus my energy on spending time with my family and in my church. I prefer to learn more about what God has planned for my family and me, and I want to learn how to lead others to Christ. These are the things that are most important, and they are the things that too many in our *noble profession* lose sight of as we become beleaguered spokespersons for the injured, forsaken, forgotten, and the damned: those injured by the acts of the reckless and neglectful.

Worth Dying For
L. Todd Kelly

We simply take on the second-hand stress of thousands of clients over time. Eventually, it beats us down until we find ourselves in some version of a closet with a 9mm pistol in our mouths.

THIS, MY FRIENDS, IS SIMPLY NOT A CAUSE WORTH DYING FOR.

I didn't stop caring about my clients. I could never do this job if I didn't care about people hurt by the carelessness, recklessness, or intent of others. I simply learned to care more, to care differently. To care about my family more, how I spend my time off more, the church more, and most importantly, to care about God more.

I started this book because I care to urge a message:

Your life has worth, even when you can't see it.

YOUR PAIN IS NOT WORTH DYING FOR.

You were….As David wrote in Psalm 23 (KJV)

The LORD is my shepherd; I shall not want.
He maketh me to lie down in green pastures:
He leadeth me beside the still waters.
He restoreth my soul:
He leadeth me in the paths of righteousness for his name's sake.

Worth Dying For
L. Todd Kelly

Yea, though I walk through the valley of the shadow of death,

I will fear no evil:

for thou art with me; Thy rod and thy staff comfort me.

Thou preparest a table before me in the presence of mine enemies:

Thou anointest my head with oil; my cup runneth over.

Surely goodness and mercy shall follow me all the days of my life:

And I will dwell in the house of the LORD forever.

Forever!

Worth Dying For
L. Todd Kelly

FATHER'S LOVE. The Father's Love does not end, though we sometimes turn our backs on Him.

FATHER'S LIFE. A Father's Life should be modeled after the life of Jesus, our Heavenly Father.

FATHER'S FEAR. A Father's Fear is unnecessary when his faith is in our Heavenly Father.

FATHER'S FIGHT. A Father's Fight is to remain righteous when temptations lead him away from God's Word.

FATHER'S WISDOM. A Father's Wisdom must be guided by The Father's Word.

THE TRUTH ABOUT SUICIDE

40

Goodbye, My Friend

My friend, you never left my heart
I always thought we'd have a start
To re-ignite our brotherhood -
That friendship was so very good.

I do not know what pain you felt;
What hurtful blow your life had dealt.
I only know it broke you down
And now they'll lay you in the ground.

You were so strong - and funny too,
My kids and I looked up to you.
We had a falling out, I know,
And so our friendship ceased to grow.

The spot you once held in my heart,
Was always yours to just restart.
I guess I now must say goodbye.
I'll never have that chance to try

Goodbye, my friend, Your absence felt
I wish I could have somehow helped.
You didn't reach. I didn't know.
The world has lost a good man, though.

Rest in Peace, my friend.

・・・・・・・・・・・・

IF I HAD PULLED that trigger rather than laying my 9mm pistol back down into the range bag in 2011, the most important chapters of this book would be blank. Of course, the book would never have been written at all. I would never have married the love of my life in front of 350 friends and family at a beautiful, rustic venue in Georgetown, Texas, in October of 2016. I would never

Worth Dying For
L. Todd Kelly

have had the chance to reconcile with Joshua, Meghan, and Matthew —or to continue to do so.

I would not know my little Jewel, Selby—this little gem would never have even existed. Her life is truly worthy!

IF I HAD PULLED THAT TRIGGER…

> I could not have gotten up to become the president of The Capital Area Trial Lawyers Association, which embraced me despite my failures.
>
> I would never have held office as a vice president of the Texas Trial Lawyers' Association.
>
> I would not have been inducted into the Texas Lawyers' Hall of Fame in 2013.
>
> I would never have been asked to serve on the Central Texas advisory committee for Mothers Against Drunk Driving.
>
> I would never have seen my name treated with any kind of respect again. I would have simply been a forgotten, failed footnote—another sad trial lawyer.

Through Grace, I now live a worthy life! If I had pulled that trigger, I could not have helped change the lives I have been privileged to help over the past decade since that day in the closet.

IF I HAD PULLED THAT TRIGGER, I COULD NOT HAVE FOUND MY WAY BACK TO JESUS

Worth Dying For
L. Todd Kelly

THE ONLY ONE WHO HAS EVER FOUND ME WORTH DYING FOR.

Since that day in the closet, I have been honored to the attorney who represented many victims of neglect and recklessness. This adds meaning to my life and requires that I draw upon power from within myself.

As of the time of this writing, I am once again stepping into firm ownership. This time, with the guidance of God and with His blessing. I am not in the same mindset as when I was young, ambitious, and foolish. I recognize today that the blessings the Lord has given me are just that—gifts. These gifts are not for me alone, but for me to share with others that the Lord loves.

OTHERS THAT HE FOUND —WORTH DYING FOR.

I still know the excruciating pain that comes from representing injured people…those who share their pain with us, and from fighting an enemy with seemingly endless resources who disregards the rules of decency and fairness. I know the personal and financial toll that each cause we bring takes. I know the hopelessness that trial lawyers feel when we do not succeed in finding justice for that client.

And I know all too well the pain of dealing with a public that maligns and hates us simply for our very existence; to then represent those same people when

Worth Dying For
L. Todd Kelly

they become the injured; and to have to plead their case to twelve people from that very group who have simply not yet become the victim—yet.

Though I know firsthand that this can be crippling and overwhelming, there is more. Get up. Find your power from within...and live your worthy life.

Japanese Kintsukuroi is the art of taking broken pottery and piecing it back together with gold. What was previously strong and useful became shattered. Then, through love and focus, it became useful again, stronger, and even more beautiful. Like those broken pieces of pottery, we can be stronger, more beautiful, and still useful if we allow God's hands to put us back together again through His power within us.

YOUR LIFE IS NOT WORTH DYING FOR...
YOU HAVE POWER WITHIN!

As I consider my role as a counselor and advocate for the clients who need me because of some tragedy that has befallen them, and the second-hand stress that accompanies that representation, I cannot help but turn my attention to my own Advocate and Counselor, who took on my entire burden when He gave His life for me on that cross. He has loved me more profoundly and sacrificed more fully to atone for my sin than any amount of stress I may have the privilege to take on for others of His children. Though I deserve to die for my countless sins, Jesus did that for me, and He will for you if you simply believe in Him. He died for you for one simple reason:

Worth Dying For
L. Todd Kelly

YOU ARE WORTH DYING FOR!

I have lost friends who did not heed my plea in this book. One of them, my Karate instructor Sean, whose pain was more than he could bear, who was externally powerful, but who failed to find the power within him at the end.

Worth Dying For
L. Todd Kelly

FATHER'S LOVE. The Father's Love redeems his children even when they feel too far gone. The Father wants each father to follow his example and is waiting for them to turn to Him.

FATHER'S LIFE. A Father's Life can be redeemed when He turns to His Heavenly Father for forgiveness and redemption.

FATHER'S FEAR. A Father's Fear is diminished when he has God with him and when he turns to Him for forgiveness and redemption.

FATHER'S FIGHT. A Father's Fight is lessened when he turns to God to help him in that fight.

FATHER'S WISDOM. A Father's Wisdom is non-existent without The Father's Word. When we try to do things on our own, we are not wise but rather foolish.

Worth Dying For
L. Todd Kelly

GOD IS NEVER LATE

41

How

*You left Your throne—
and man, you served,
To wear a crown that I
deserved.
We failed to treat You as
our King,
And at our hands, You felt
death's sting.*

*You pleaded, cried – tears
in Your eyes,
For You knew that You
would hear our cries.
Now many turn to You in
vain,
And beg You to relieve
their pain.*

*You breathed Your last.
The veil was torn,
By Your pure love – a
pathway born.
Defeating death, You rose
again,
To wash away my very
sin.*

*Thank you, Father for all
You've done,
For sending us Your only
Son,
That when we turn to
Him and ask,
Our sins He takes – His
promised task.*

*You carry off my heavy
load,
And lead me down that
narrow road.
The one You paved for
those who will
Answer "yes," and follow
still.*

*You rose to sit at the right
of God
And walk where only
Angels trod.
The glory Yours, the
power, too
Father, we sing praise to
You.*

*We praise You for the
fight you've won,
The victory of your slain
Son,
But praise also for
Amazing Grace,
That removed my sin
without a trace.*

*I don't deserve – and
never will,
But as Your promises,
You fulfill,
I live again in freedom
now!
Thank you, Father—
You're the "how."*

Worth Dying For
L. Todd Kelly

AS MEN AND WOMEN with limited ability to see the ripple effects of what we do, we often do not understand the import. As I sat on the floor of my closet—ready to take my own life because of my failures—I could never have known that the case and our work would ever make any positive difference. It seemed I had merely fought a losing battle that cost me everything and produced nothing but additional pain for my client and friend, Jamie.

I am a long-time member of the AAJ (American Association for Justice). The AAJ supported my efforts in the litigation when Jamie and I pursued justice and worked to change the laws to prohibit mandatory, binding arbitration provisions in employment contracts.

Our position has remained that these provisions violate the 7th Amendment to the United States Constitution, which by its language, guarantees that the right to a civil trial in disputes over $20 shall not be infringed. November 4, 2021: I was sitting at an awards ceremony during a conference of the Texas Trial Lawyers Association in San Antonio, Texas when I received an email from my friend, Vicki Slater, a leader at the American Association for Justice from Mississippi. That email read:

> *The Senate Judiciary Committee just approved a bill to end forced arbitration in the sexual harassment/sexual assault claims by a unanimous voice vote!!!!!! This bill is entirely bi-partisan and has an excellent chance of passing both Houses and onto the President's desk. Republican Senators Graham, Grassley, Blackburn, Kennedy, and Hawley*

Worth Dying For
L. Todd Kelly

asked to be original co-sponsors of the bill and all the Senate Democrats.

This bill results from much shoe leather expended by the Women's Trial Lawyer Caucus of AAJ on the Hill during Lobby Days and the AAJ staff.

But I would be remiss if I didn't mention the F Warrior who began this fight with his wonderful client Jamie. Todd, please tell her about this. You and Jaime shined the glaring light of justice on the evils of forced arbitration in a way that still resonates in the halls of Congress and will now resonate in courthouses around the land. You didn't win the fight in court, my friend, but few lawyers get victories as large as this. You have transformed the landscape and opened the courthouse doors for thousands.

I'm in awe.

You two will always be heroes in my eyes.

Love
Vicki Slater
Attorney at Law, P.A.

••••••••••••

Tears welled in my eyes as I recalled the jury sending us home in *defeat*.

I recalled the look of disbelief in Jamie's eyes.

I again felt those days alone in my darkness...

...and I remembered the cold, metallic taste of that Beretta in my Mouth.

Worth Dying For
L. Todd Kelly

But I remembered something else.

I remembered why I wanted to take on this corporate giant in the first place and why Jamie asked me to to change the law for the better.

It came over me in waves. After more than a decade, while Jamie would never be compensated for her suffering; while my team would never be paid for their dedication, hard work, and personal risk; and while my law firm would not be restored; I now know that we didn't lose at all that day. We had actually done something big and changed the law for the better! We had done something that made life worth living.

More than a decade after sitting in that closet in disgrace and shame, ready to take my own life under the weight of that shame and my feelings of worthlessness. The same group of people that I was too ashamed to lift my head to face sent messages to me like the following:

Congratulations to everyone involved in this Moosecaller

Regards,
Paul R. Dumas, Jr., Esq.

••••••••••

Worth Dying For
L. Todd Kelly

And today here's L. Todd Kelly, showing the world how to make a Lotus bloom from the mud of suffering.

Thank you for your hard work, contribution and courage to snatch victory from the jaws of adversity, my friend.

Chris

•••••••••••

This is incredible! Thank you, Todd!!

Love,

Cherie Trine

•••••••••••

Yes. This is a tremendous victory to all involved in this historic step in fighting for justice. Thank you to all

V. Iyer

•••••••••••

Outstanding work from a lawyer that cares!

Frederick "Rick" I. Hall, III

•••••••••••

Worth Dying For
L. Todd Kelly

Two of THE bravest people I know. Bar none.

V----

••••••••••••

It is telling of my brother and sister's trial lawyers that these congratulatory accolades are not in response to a significant monetary verdict but about the positive change that was accomplished.

These simple email messages reveal the true heart of the American Trial Lawyer.

> JUSTICE AND GOODNESS ARE OUR TRUE NORTH;
> MONEY DOES NOT CHANGE THAT.

Though we did not know it then, God took what Jamie and I started and worked through other hands to complete the work in a way we could not have imagined or completed on our own. I post these emails here not for self-gratification (though there is ample joy in receiving them) but to show God's work's redeeming power when we agree to follow Him.

Worth Dying For
L. Todd Kelly

FATHER'S LOVE. A Father's Love is never-ending and patient. When we follow the example of the Heavenly Father, our patience and depth of love are even more.

FATHER'S LIFE. A Father's Life is supportive and comforting to his children and family.

FATHER'S FEAR. A Father's Fear should be of God alone.

FATHER'S FIGHT. A Father's Fight is for his family, but there will be other fights.

FATHER'S WISDOM. A Father's Wisdom is demonstrated by passing his love of God to his family.

THE HEART OF FATHERS

42

THE GREATEST DAD

As a dad, we have to be much more
Than just a man our kids adore.
For if we fail to keep God's trust
Our babies turn to greed and lust.

To father is more than just to sire,
That is done of pure desire.
But to be the dad we're called to be,
Requires that we bend a knee.

Look to the Father of us all,
If fatherhood is to be your call.

He shows us how to love a child,
Just as He: both strong and mild.

Turn not to work or life's distractions
When you are called to take some action,
Rather turn your children to,
The one who gave their care to you.

Remember that His heart is pure,
You will fail, but can endure,
Just repent and turn back in,
And let Him hold you once again.

••••••••••••

THE TRUTH IS WE learn what is worth dying for from our Father, whether earthly or Heavenly. Our Fathers instill in us right and wrong, our worth and potential, and what we should and should not accept. Fathers play a far more critical role in our lives and the social construct.

Maybe you had a great father here on earth. Maybe you didn't. But the simple fact is we all need one, and men, we can all be one. We can be *fathers* to the kids we coach. We can be *fathers* to the young person just starting with your company. We can be "fathers" to our wives and heal the wounds that other men have created in their lives. And we can be "fathers" to our fellow friends.

The heart of the father goes far beyond biology and age. The heart of the father taps into your bravery, undying love, commitment, valor, and stoic courage that our society needs and so many people seek.

IN YOUR CAREER it means putting integrity before income, and truth over image. Trust God to take care of you, and lead by showing Him to your colleagues, clients and customers.

IN YOUR HOME it means doing the right thing even when your children can't see you. This is a bit of a rhetorical statement because sooner or later, they always see you. God rewards those who are faithful to him. Display that sense of encouragement to your children and watch as they are blessed as well.

IN YOUR RELATIONSHIPS it means to honor God's word. I have failed in this area so many times that I have lost count, but God is forgiving. Start today. Treat others with love and encouragement. Display the love of Christ, as He commanded, and watch your relationships blossom. But also, be wise in whom you choose to invest your time. God is also clear on this—surround yourself with those who sharpen you, as you

Worth Dying For
L. Todd Kelly

in turn sharpen them.

IN YOUR SELF it means to know who you are in Him. He found you worth dying for in the most excruciating way imaginable. Just hold that in for a moment.

YOU ARE WORTH DYING FOR —TO THE KING OF THE UNIVERSE.

Honor that death and that humility that He bore for you by being worth it to Him.

Because when we step up and into our father-hearts, we step into the divine we are called to. We step into loving not just the Church but all of humanity the way Christ did. We step into the biological protectors we are designed to be. We step into what our hearts seek as a life fulfilled, and we fulfill the needs of the people around us as well.

Let me be frank. The lies society has told you and me as men for the last five decades are lies. The heart of the Father —both heavenly and through us here on earth—is needed, wanted, and desired.

Don't shrink back.
Don't get distracted.
Don't pretend that you don't matter.
Don't fall for the social allure.

Worth Dying For
L. Todd Kelly

You are fully equipped.
You are fully capable.
You are fully prepared.

    And your heavenly Father is there to be the father you need and show you how to lead here on earth.

    As I have outlined in this work, it is easy to produce offspring, but raising children is so much more. Particularly to raise the children of God, which is what we are all called to do. Jesus showed us that love when he paid the price for our sins so that we could spend eternity with Him in Heaven.

    It seems so obvious that as earthly dads we will pay the way for our children—at least until their 18th birthdays. That is actually enforced by law in most U.S. jurisdictions. This payment for our children was modeled by our Savior when he took the death that we all deserved. He did that for me, for you, and for our children. But even after we are through paying for their way, we must continue to PAVE the way. We are able do this through our continued love and commitment by setting the example for our children to follow—even when they do not appear to want to.

    How many times do we hear about how much it costs to raise a child in today's society?

    How much did it cost my Heavenly Father to raise (and save) me?

Worth Dying For
L. Todd Kelly

From that perspective, what I pay to raise my own children (both financially and in terms of time investment) are minuscule.

The decision to have children should never be made lightly. Once that commitment has been undertaken, then a father has the obligation to dedicate his life to raising those children as God has commanded that they be raised. His life must be an example to those children in order to provide them with the knowledge and strength to eventually raise their own children to fear and love our Heavenly Father.

Children will stray from the guidance of their parents. Have we not all strayed from the commands of our Heavenly Father? The important thing is that the parents use the proper leadership and guidance to reign them back in so that they are the Christ-followers that we are commanded to raise. When I stray (even when it is as far away from God as the walks I took in this book), I have been brought back into God's redemption only because He opened the door and showed me the way, sometimes when I didn't even want to walk it. This, we must do for our own children as well: leave them a way to repent and —just as Jesus has left that door open to you. Follow God's own example.

As fathers to our children, we must fight the influence of the world over their impressionable lives. Yet, we must do it with love so as to show the power of Love and the truth of our message. Jesus exemplified this when he was here among us by loving even those

Worth Dying For
L. Todd Kelly

who mocked and crucified him. Our children will experience feelings of anger, even hatred, toward others. It is our responsibility to ensure that their emotions, their actions, and their hearts do not turn from the teachings of our Lord.

Wisdom, they say, is often gained from experience. In my case, I had to experience soul-crushing losses to finally repent of my sinful ways and start to seek forgiveness from God. My sin did not stop that day, and because I am human, it does not ever truly end. My prayer is that, through the power of the Holy Spirit, I sin less and less each day, and that He washes me clean so that I may be presentable to the Lord when that day comes.

I have learned that wisdom does not come from books (except the Holy Bible) and it does not come from the things of the world. Knowledge may come from these sources, but wisdom comes from the Lord, and it is therefore only He who can choose the wise. The wisest man (short of Jesus) to have ever lived became wise as a favor from God when that was his prayer.

Solomon's wisdom was not because of his intellect or his study, but from God, because he trusted. That is the Power Within each of us, if we seek the Holy Spirit.

AND IT WAS OUR FATHER WHO WANTED TO MAKE US WISE AND TO BRING US HOME WITH HIM WHO SHOWED US WHAT WAS TRULY WORTH DYING FOR.

Worth Dying For
L. Todd Kelly

FATHER'S LOVE. The Father's Love provides safety, but also reproach of wrongdoing.

FATHER'S LIFE. A Father's Life must be an example that leads to Jesus.

FATHER'S FEAR. A Father's Fear is that his children do not learn the lessons he has for them so that they live a better life. Much like our Heavenly Father's fear, we reject what He has taught.

FATHER'S FIGHT. A Father's Fight is against the ways of this world, that his Children turn to Jesus for salvation and for strength, rather than to depend upon the world for those things.

FATHER'S WISDOM: A Father's Wisdom comes only from the Lord. The wise know where to seek it.

Worth Dying For
L. Todd Kelly

FATHER'S LOVE. The Father's Love provides safety, but also reproach of wrongdoing.

FATHER'S LIFE. A Father's Life must be an example that leads to Jesus.

FATHER'S FEAR. A Father's Fear is that his children do not learn the lessons he has for them so that they live a better life. Much like our Heavenly Father's fear, we reject what He has taught.

FATHER'S FIGHT. A Father's Fight is against the ways of this world, that his Children turn to Jesus for salvation and for strength, rather than to depend upon the world for those things.

FATHER'S WISDOM: A Father's Wisdom comes only from the Lord. The wise know where to seek it.

About The Author

With a protector's heart, L. Todd Kelly mesmerizes audiences big and small around the world. Being a sought-after trial lawyer and media commentator, Kelly knows how to grab the hearts and minds of any audience.

Beginning his law practice in the U.S. Marine Corps, Kelly's career has protected victims in all backgrounds and social statuses.

Kelly and the cases he has represented have been seen on The Rachel Maddow Show, The New York Times, Wall Street Journal, CNN, NBC, and FOX. Bold, unapologetic, and a true fighter—Kelly knows what it takes to succeed personally and professionally.

In 2024 Kelly reopened The Kelly Law Firm as Lone Star Legal where he is senior partner. Married to his loving wife, Robbye, the couple has a daughter, Selby Jewel; they spend time almost weekly with Todd's other children, Joshua, Meghan, and Matthew.

MOST NOTABLY, KELLY IS A CHILD OF A LOVING, FORGIVING GOD WHO FOUND HIM
 WORTH DYING FOR

To learn more about Kelly's law firm go to https://lonestarlegal.com and to book Kelly as a speaker please go to https://www.ltoddkelly.com/

L. Todd Kelly Speaks

Dynamic, powerful, and mindset shifting—L. Todd Kelly's open candor about career, kids, and the stress that it all can take on a person makes him a sought-after speaker for corporate organizations and industry associations.

Because of his diverse background and direct nature, Kelly connects with audiences large and small allowing him to truly speak to the hearts and minds of these c-suite level professionals. No matter if he is main stage speaker or part of an intimate fireside chat experience—Kelly is able to make all attendees feel like he is speaking directly to them and their personal experience.

To book Kelly for your next event, please go to https://www.ltoddkelly.com/

www.ingramcontent.com/pod-product-compliance
Lightning Source LLC
Chambersburg PA
CBHW051622010526
44119CB00039B/476/J